Now I Am Free

LINDA LANG

BALBOA PRESS

A DIVISION OF HAY HOUSE

Balboa Press books may be ordered through booksellers or by contacting:

Balboa Press
A Division of Hay House
1663 Liberty Drive
Bloomington, IN 47403
www.balboapress.com.au
1-(877) 407-4847

ISBN: 978-1-4525-0615-9 (sc)
ISBN: 978-1-4525-0616-6 (e)

Because of the dynamic nature of the Internet, any web addresses or links contained in this book may have changed since publication and may no longer be valid. The views expressed in this work are solely those of the author and do not necessarily reflect the views of the publisher, and the publisher hereby disclaims any responsibility for them.

The author of this book does not dispense medical advice or prescribe the use of any technique as a form of treatment for physical, emotional, or medical problems without the advice of a physician, either directly or indirectly. The intent of the author is only to offer information of a general nature to help you in your quest for emotional and spiritual well-being. In the event you use any of the information in this book for yourself, which is your constitutional right, the author and the publisher assume no responsibility for your actions.

Any people depicted in stock imagery provided by Thinkstock are models, and such images are being used for illustrative purposes only.
Certain stock imagery © Thinkstock.

Printed in the United States of America

Balboa Press rev. date: 07/23/2012

Contents

The Power of Intentions

The year 2009 reverberated with every emotion and every dream I'd ever had screaming through the ether, swirling around me faster and faster, until I thought that I would fall out of my chair. I clung to its sides to keep me on the seat as tears flowed freely down my cheeks. I could taste the saltiness as they touched my lips and followed the line of my mouth to my tongue. It was the sweetest thing I had ever experienced. The magic that Esther Hicks spoke as she transformed into words the emotions she received from Abraham flowed like a breeze around the room. It became sound, entering my ears and sending shivers of exquisite resonance flowing through every cell of my body and into the very core of my being.

At last the endless searching, asking, and reaching for had brought me to this place where so many people were gathered. I could feel the vibration of all those wonderful souls sending out tentacles of energy and light, reaching towards the stage where Esther stood like a lightning rod, attracting the tentacles to come ever closer. My heart was beating so fast, and I turned towards my husband to say something, though I am not quite sure what. He too had tears of joy in his eyes and the most beautiful smile I had ever seen. He was there with me in this wonderful place of enlightenment and empowerment.

In Appreciation

To Louise Hay, Dr. Wayne Dyer, Deepak Chopra, John Assaraf, Bob Proctor, and Esther and Jerry Hicks. You have devoted so much of your time to mentor thousands of people all around the world. You have been our teachers for eighteen years, and we love and appreciate you enormously. Thanks. We are refreshed.

To my wonderful husband, who supported me through all the healing. You kept your hand firmly under the elbow of my soul as I wrote this book and dealt with all the old demons again. I love you beyond words and thank you once again for our beautiful son, who has been an inspiration to us both. (The teacher of teachers.) To our son for your support and unconditional love at all times, even when the vortex sometimes spits us out. Thank you, Cookie, for teaching Mama and Dada so many wonderful things. You are the greatest little manifester we know.

To my three older sons, thanks for loving me and never placing conditions on that love. Thanks for your support throughout the years when we shared a home and for all the fun times we had. I appreciate the times when you were there for me, when things got too much for me to bear. I love you, my darlings, and want you to know that I have always seen your magnificence and greatness from the days each of you were born. A mum could never have asked for better children to share her time with. You have inspired me to write this book

Namaste

The Law of Attraction in Action

The law of attraction is universal, and every person is affected by it. It is always true that what you think, what you feel, and what you get is always a match. There is not one single person on this planet that was unaware of this fact when he or she was born, and there is not a person on this planet that would not benefit by knowing it.

The law of attraction is the basis of everything you see, everything you are, and everything that has or is coming into your life. Having awareness and understanding of how the law of attraction works is paramount to living your life of purpose, living the life you came here to live. What does it all mean? It's simple. That which is like unto itself is drawn; what you believe will in fact mold and create the story of your reality.

Every time you talk to someone you hear the words "the law of attraction," "the secret," and "vibrational expansion." The words are on the lips of so many people. The questions are flying around the universe. What's happening? How come no one said anything before? Or have people been talking about this since time memorial? There is an eagerness to be a part of this new time-space reality that we find ourselves in. It is very exciting and tremendously enlightening.

Everyone wants to know how they can take advantage of living in a state of awareness and empowerment. How can they change the life of the mundane into a life of fulfillment and joyfulness? All of these questions were ones that haunted me for many years while I was locked away from society in an orphanage.

As I got older I became more persistent. I rebelled against what I had been taught. There just seemed to be no point in being alive if it was ordained that we just let go and allow other people to have total control over our lives.

There had to be more. It was only a matter of time before all was revealed to me in such a simple manner. It took my breath away for one moment and then breathed life back into me, and I came alive for the first time in forty years. My powers of perception changed, and I felt as if I had been handed the most precious gift of all. Freedom!

Irrespective of what everyone else is telling you about what they see as your life so far, leave them to their own conclusions and make a concerted effort to love who you are now. Open your mind and step outside of the box. Beyond yourself is all that you could ever want, and more, waiting to be experienced. Allow the magnificence of life to permeate your very existence and set you free.

You are source energy. You are a most powerful and wonderful human being who came here for the express purpose to have fun and a joyful life. Do it!

Once you have become aware of who you really are and your purpose on this earth, there is no turning back. So be you. Love who you are and go forth into this world, matching up with everything that you are and all that you have become through your asking.

The most important goal you need to set yourself is learning how to love yourself. The relationship that needs to be of the highest priority is the one between you and you. Everything else is irrelevant to your personal growth and expansion.

Come with me on a journey into the past, where I first learnt about God, limitations, and pain, and then follow me into a world so beautiful and empowering, you too will wonder why someone never told you before.

CHAPTER 1
Locked Memories

As I look to the sky and hear the sound of a lonely bird cry. I feel the emptiness that within me lies as my memories slip into the abyss where nothing lives. I am alone. Linda Lang

I HAVE THIS RECURRING dream. Nothing fearful or untoward happens, but I have been to this place in my dreams since I was a child. Was it a dream, or is there some latent reason that I have experienced this journey over and over for as long as I can remember?

I walk along a road; it is unpaved and dry. To my right are some housing units. They are two floors high and have no distinguishing features except that they are built of rust-colored bricks. I stand in front of them, yet I see no entrances. There are no doors and no stairs to reach the top. There are no people that I can see, and yet I know someone is in there. All the curtains are closed, and they all look just the same. Nothing has any color except those bricks.

On the left side of the road is a vacant lot. It is covered in long grass with small bushes dotted around. The bushes are dry and twiggy.

I continue up the road, away from the units, since this seems to be the only way to proceed. There are no other paths, so I just continue to follow the road aimlessly, looking straight ahead, seeing nothing but the road. There is an awareness within me that there are other houses along the way, but I do not see them.

I am there. I am standing in front of an old gate. A path leads to a house that is the only building on the land. It is situated far off the road but directly in front of me. The path appears to be an old, worn track cutting through the grass and directly up to the house.

The large expanse of grass has no definite color and covers the ground, although there is a shrub to the right of the path. Actually, it is more like a tree whose growth has been stunted through years of neglect.

I stand there. I have no compulsion to go into the house or stay out. I just feel neutral. The house is light-colored with light-green trim; it is raised about two feet off the ground and looks like an old timber house. It is very ordinary, with no outstanding features.

Steps lead up to a small landing where the front door is located. There is a sort of arch above the door, but it is slightly distorted and unappealing. The door seems to be of no consequence, yet I am compelled to stare at it with a deep longing in my heart.

Is this my life? Is there an explanation for this dream? All I know is that I have had this dream throughout my life. I have visited this house more times in my dream than I can remember actually living in one.

I lived in an orphanage for most of my young life, starting at the age of four. The honest truth is I cannot remember much of my life, but what I do recall; I want to share with you.

I know that what I have to tell you will be of tremendous benefit to you. All you have to do is read this book objectively and without prejudice. Do not feel sad or pity me. Just celebrate my newfound freedom to be able to put into words my story of empowerment.

A Brief Synopsis

I was born in the early fifties. My mother was married to a man who constantly beat her. According to her, he seemed to adore me and was neutral towards my brother. My brother was two years younger than I, and neither of us really remembers our father.

We all lived with my grandmother, who was actually my mother's adoptive mother. I heard is a story about a girl who once worked in my grandparents' home. My grandfather took advantage of her and she got pregnant soon after the affair began.

When her pregnancy was discovered, she was given her walking papers. No one is sure why she felt compelled to leave the child behind. She just disappeared and was never seen again. My grandfather died in the forties, so my grandmother raised the child—my mother—as a single parent. My grandmother died when I was three years old, and I don't have any memories of her.

I make no judgment or comment about my biological grandmother, as I never walked in her shoes. I reserve the right to mind my own business, leave others to their devices, and focus on my life's journey.

My mother tells me that my grandmother was a woman of strong character and bodily strength. On one occasion after my father hit my mother, my grandmother punched him so hard, he flew over the couch and almost out the front door. I don't think my mother saw the humor in that at the time, but if she did, who could really blame her?

According to my mother, my grandmother doted on me and would take me with her wherever she went. She would spend her last dime on me; and even though she was in her sixties, she would carry me all the way home if I fell asleep. She must have been a very special woman, and I suspect I take after her in strength and character.

From the time I was four, I grew up in one orphanage after another, at the whim of the social welfare system. When my mother and father separated we lived with my mother who is a gentle and loving soul. According to my mother, I was taken away because my father had informed the welfare office that she was unfit to be a mother. I was removed from this secure and loving environment and sent to an orphanage, my brother was placed in the custody of my mother's best friend. At the time, my mother was carrying her third child. When he was born, he too was removed from the home, and she was forced to give him up for adoption.

CHAPTER 2
Who Turned Out the Lights?

I am the sheep, but where is the shepherd? I wander around searching for my herd, but all I see is desolation and abandonment.
Linda Cameron

I RECALL THAT THE first orphanage I was placed in was a strict religious institution. The few memories I have are not pleasant ones. I recall that when I was first taken there, the place seemed so dark. It made me think it was built out of the darkest timber that had had all the life and warmth squeezed out of it. A set of stairs led up to the dormitories where we all slept. When I looked up the stairs, they seemed to disappear into a deep, gaping hole that had no end.

It was a cold place, and no one seemed to have a smile for me. There was no gentle hand; there were no kind words. I was just led up the stairs into that dark hole and taken to a room where I was shown my bed. The bed was so high, and I wondered how I was going to get up onto it. The room was light, but it was lifeless and unwelcoming. Everything was white, almost blinding to the eyes. Nothing was out of place, and there was not a single splash of color.

I had a small paper package, and it contained my clothes and everything in the world that I owned. There were no toys in that package. As I stood there unsure what to do, a strange claw like hand suddenly reached out and snatched the bag from me, and then disappeared.

I was alone, confused, and very afraid. I felt as if someone had tied a band around my throat and was pulling it tighter and tighter. No matter how hard I swallowed, I could not dislodge the lump that was growing in my throat and cutting off my air supply.

Where was my mother? I did not even have a clear memory of the person who had dropped me off. I wondered then if it mattered. It did matter once I got older, and I began to understand the implications of where my life seemed to be going.

In the meantime, I was in this place—a nothing, a nobody of less consequence than the time of day. There had been other children outside, and they hadn't batted an eyelash at the newcomer. Was I the only one who felt she was in a dark tunnel, or did the other children feel the same way?

Tears ran down my face. I felt lost, without hope. My rock was gone. Where was my mother? Why couldn't I see her? Was she feeling as I did? Had she held my hand and then passed me over to these people who seemed so cold and disinterested?

I kept repeating this in my mind: *I am so sorry, Mommy, if I did something to hurt you. I promise I will always be good from now on. Please come and take me home. I love you.*

I could see myself looking around in a panic, as if I were outside my body. The walls almost looked like they were crying, or did those tears belong to me? I felt like I was drowning. *Please, someone save me! I want to go home.*

Today, I have nothing left of this place but the occasional memory.

One of those memories is of the debilitating experience I had when I wet my bed for the first time. I was confused and so afraid. Upon awakening at 6:00 a.m., I tried to cover up the damp sheet, not sure of the reaction I was going to get. I think one of the other kids saw me and reported it to the sister. Oh, horror! I was unceremoniously taken by the ear and, with my feet barely touching the ground, hauled off to the bathroom.

Oh, I remember that large scrubbing brush as if it just happened yesterday. It was the one they used to scrub the floor. The smell of disinfectant was overwhelming, and my skin was raw and tender for days afterwards.

Once I was dressed, the sister tied the wet pajama pants around my neck, and that was how I had to attend breakfast. A lot of kids made comments about my smell and what I had done. Children can be so cruel in their innocence.

After breakfast I had to wash the sheets and a card with my name printed on it was pinned to the sheets for all to see. This experience had a profound effect on me, and I continued to wet my bed until I was nine years old.

How does one lose the memories of so many painful years? I remember being locked in a cupboard at the bottom of the stairs, the swings in the yard, being hit on the knuckles with a wooden ruler for biting my nails, and being told to fear and love God above all else.

Not much to look forward to, wouldn't you agree? Did I go to school outside those gates? Who knows? I do recall being taken to a place where the staff observed us through a window, but not much else. There was never any kindness or outings that I can recall. If this all I had to relate to as I grew up, should I not have become a cold and unfeeling child?

Goodness knows how one does develop a strong character and personality when so much of her childhood is wiped away. No memories of joy or laughter. How does a child build any kind of relationship with other people, let alone herself?

I remember my fear of contact with certain staff members at the orphanage, and how uncomfortable I was for years, even after I had left school. I was always looking over my shoulder, certain I was being followed. I was fearful of looking at the bedroom door at night and was never able to turn off the lights to go to sleep. These feeling were so menacing, and I always felt out of control and weak.

Am I that house in my dream that just stands there, with no one ever entering it? Am I lost forever in a void of nothingness? No love, no warmth, no tenderness, and no mother. I don't even remember my mother visiting me or holding me. Where the hell was everyone? Why had this happened to me?

A Place of No Hope

I am like a blind man lost in a field of tall grass, a labyrinth of never ending pathways that lead to nowhere. There was no one to show me the way out, just a void and the need to shout. Linda Lang

I have searched every avenue for an explanation, and never at any time have I felt I would reach a better understanding of my situation. As I grew up, I never gained any clarity about what had happened and why.

No one I knew spoke about it. It was almost as if it did not happen. Silence and aloofness were my only companions day after day, year after year.

How easily we place our trust in adults, even when there is no affection or love. We just believe what they say and take guidance from them, which become our belief systems and the foundation on which we build our lives.

Oh, I asked the questions. Why? Who is responsible? What did I do wrong? Why was God punishing me? Could I change my situation? Would my life continue along these lines until I died? Was this a book that had been written and set in concrete? Did I really choose to be in this place of pain and confusion? I might have been only four, but I was already thinking like an adult. I was asking questions that even now make no sense to most adults I talk to.

I clearly remember the answer I got when I asked the strangers who looked after me, "Why am I here? What did I do?" They told me it was God who decided who got what and who went where. No choices, only subservience and obedience.

It is amazing how certain words and events stay with you, almost as if they are waiting for the day you put pen to paper. Then they suddenly pour out, a flood of words and feelings, like a huge wave of water pouring forth and knocking you off your feet.

You feel like you are drowning. Your emotions are so close to the surface as the branches and twigs tear painfully at your skin, ripping at you as if to tear your heart out of its protective pocket. You try to claw your way back to the surface, reaching for the sunlight so as to prevent yourself from falling again into the abyss of despair. Why?

As each moment of my life unfolds, I have been searching for the answers, seeking input from those who are more in the know than I. I asked God over and over, without knowing how to listen if there was any answer. After all, my understanding was that God only spoke to saints and priests. What chance did I stand of any communication at all?

I remained in that orphanage of No Hope, as I dubbed it, with so many other lost and abandoned children. Was it the parents' fault, the welfare agency's fault, or had we as children asked in some mysterious way to be placed in these situations?

Had we done something wrong in a past life, had it been preordained by God, or did we actually have some say in the matter?

As you can see, I had so many unanswered questions and I was developing a whole lot of theories from a new perspective. But I digress. There is a long way to go until all can be revealed. I can feel the winds of change becoming a little gusty even as I write this book. Things are no longer as black and white and set in concrete as I had first thought.

My journey of renewal and release is about to begin, as I have gradually allowed myself the right to let it all out. To share with you the story of a life that may or may not make sense to you. Ultimately, it may help you throw open the doors of your own personal prison and break free of the chains that hold you bondage.

CHAPTER 3

Time to Move On

Despair is what keeps me alive; it's my companion to help me survive.
Linda Lang

MOST OF THE CHILDREN in that particular orphanage were there only until they turned six or seven, and then they were forwarded on to another home, as was I. Once again, all the old familiar faces took on new masklike features. Did they change overnight, or did someone come stealthily in the middle of the night and paint new faces on them?

I arrived at the new home just before I turned seven, since I was getting ready to start school. This place was bigger and more central to town.

The new faces looked like they were etched out of stone. The woman in charge had lifeless eyes. The deep creases alongside her mouth turned it down, sort of like an upside-down smile. The lines on her forehead seemed to take on a life of their own as she frowned at me and gripped my arm in a steely grip.

When she spoke to me, her mouth moved in an almost comical way, opening and closing over the words like puppets in the Punch and Judy show. She was called Matron, and her staff stood behind her with blank stares. She handed me over to one of the staff, and I remember thinking that she acted as though

I was a bottle of soda on an assembly line that needed to be moved from one position to the next.

I was taken up the stairs to my dormitory. There were dormitories both upstairs and downstairs. Each section had its own showers and toilets.

There was a gigantic communal dining room where we also occasionally watched movies. The grounds were enormous and gently sloping. When I looked out the window of my dormitory room, I could see a large tree and a set of swings. There were no children at the home when I arrived, as they were already at school.

As with the other home, everything was white and sterile. The dormitory floor shone like glass, and in it I could see the outline of a girl as she slowly walked to the window and looked out. It was I, but I was detached from myself and everything that was going on.

"Do hurry," the staff member who'd brought me there said. "Matron will be waiting, and she does not take kindly to people who waste her time."

I turned around and looked at the woman. Strangely, she seemed as fearful as I felt.

Each dormitory room had twenty beds with small bedside tables between them. The beds were steel frames with a hard mattress covered in starched sheets and a white cotton blanket. All of our clothes were taken from us and placed in the linen room on a shelf. Each morning a staff member gave us our clothes to wear that day. I wondered why they would remove all personal things from us. It was as if we had just become a number, and this added to the insult of our nonbeing.

Before bedtime that first night, I was given a pair of pajamas, my toothbrush, and a comb. These were to be my closest companions while I was in that home. I cried like a baby that night, because I had been taken from children whom I had come to accept as my family. Although none of us formed any true bonds, the children at that first home were familiar to me and I had come to understand their aloofness to some degree.

No matter how many years had passed, I still longed for the comfort and warmth of my mother's arms. The memory was fast fading, and I would lie awake at night thinking the memory back into existence. I just wanted that moment more than I wanted to be alive. It was the last memory I had before I fell asleep at night for many years to come.

I could not understand why I was being punished so much, and try as I might, I could not fathom the thinking behind the orphanages that children were forced to live in. Was there something I could do or say to God that would let him know that this was not the way to treat those you loved? But then, what did I know? It was all I had become accustomed to over the past three years. How the memories fade as new ones are learnt.

School, Sunday school, and church, no matter where I went, they told me everything that happened to me was God's will. I was told never to question God, as he would not take kindly to that. He could do anything he wanted, and my life could get worse. But what could be worse than this?

Oh no, please, God, not again. I had wet the bed, and on my first night there. After my impression of Matron and my inability to talk to any of the other kids on my first day there, it did not bode well for me. Some of the girls laughed nervously at me as someone went to call Matron.

Ouch! That hurt. Matron had grabbed me by the ear, and as she dragged me off to the bathroom, she kept repeating, "You are nothing but trouble. I could see that from the first moment you got here. For the life of me I don't understand why you weren't aborted at birth. Why do these young tramps insist on bring children into a world that has nothing to offer anyone?"

This woman was one angry person, and now she had me at her mercy. I was terrified. Thank goodness I did not get a scrubbing, but I had to wash my sheets, put my mattress outside, and place my name on it for all to see.

This was so humiliating, and once again I became a laughingstock. Once again even the kids who were not in my dormitory got to see that I had wet my bed. I hated everyone, they were all mean, and I wished they would all go to hell.

My first day in my new "home" had started off as a nightmare. I prayed so hard and earnestly to God that day, asking for help with not wetting the bed, as I went through the motions of being introduced to the headmaster of my school. I met my teacher and new classmates, and then the world went blank for the remainder of that day.

The last thing I remembered before I fell asleep that night was the muffled sobs that reached my ears and mingled with mine. In that room I realized that each and every one of those girls was afraid and in so much despair.

I made a vow to myself that I would not wet the bed and fell asleep. I continued to wet my bed for the duration of my two-year stay there, and so I became more and more withdrawn and was teased mercilessly while I remained incarcerated in that place for children.

On one particular night after all the kids had settled in for the night, Matron came into the room as she usually did before lights out. She walked past the foot of each bed and never said a word. Suddenly I heard her explosive words: "Get those hands out of there, you filthy little ingrate. What are you doing under there? Take those disgusting hands out and place them on top of the blankets."

She looked at me as if I was vermin, and I don't think I have ever moved so fast in my life. My hands were on the blankets, and even I looked at them as if they were a curse. What had they been doing that was so bad? They had just been lying along my sides, my hands holding onto my thighs.

Maybe thighs were evil and dirty. I would remember that for a long time, to keep my hands away from all parts of my body, unless I was washing. And then it had to so quick and impersonal, making sure never to look at my body in a mirror.

It seemed God had created woman as an afterthought and we were the lowest of his creations. To look at or touch our bodies was, without a doubt, vain and sinful.

I am not here to defend or berate the Christian religion, merely to give you an insight into why I needed to get answers to my questions. I have read and reread the Bible many times, often quite shocked by the violence and obscenity within its pages. Throughout the entire time I spent in orphanages, I too experienced much horror, greed, and jealousy but never as much as I experienced while reading that book.

We were forced to reread the Bible over and over, learning verses until we could recite large sections of it by heart. I learnt to read very well from an early age and was also a brilliant speller.

My days started out the same every day. I had by then made a new friend. She had the most beautiful hair and green eyes that sparkled in spite of where she was. We had become firm friends and also shared the same dormitory. Having a friend made life there more bearable and not quite so lonely.

One day I took the dog that belonged to one of the staff for a walk. I'll call him DJ. We walked along the fence line that formed a border between the orphanage and the outside world.

The fence had sharp steel pickets on top that looked like arrows. A thick hedge grew over the fence, and DJ and I were inside that hedge. I was on top of the picket fence, balancing over the pickets.

One foot in front of the other, I shakily balanced my weight, taking great care with my footing so as not to slip and fall. Suddenly I heard someone call my name, and in my haste to get back to the orphanage, I placed my foot on top of one of the pickets. As the metal touched my foot, I recoiled and fell on top of the pickets.

The pain was unbearable as the point of the picket entered my buttock and hit the bone. I thought I would die. I stumbled out of the hedge and straight into Matron, who had been calling me.

My poor bottom cheek was bleeding so badly. As I stood before her with blood everywhere, Matron looked furious. She already hated me so much, and I was sure life was about to get worse for me. I was taken to the nursing station and patched up.

The Doctor said that I didn't need stitches and that I hadn't broken anything. Good thing they had X-ray eyes. I was sent to bed without dinner, as a child of the devil like me did not deserve to eat with the other kids according to Matron.

After I'd been there for four months, one of the staff told me that my mother and aunt had been granted permission to come see me. I was elated, afraid and nervous all at the same time. It had been so long since I had seen my mommy, and I had not seen my brother since I was four years old. Since then, my mother had had another child whom I had never met.

The day when my mother and aunt arrived was very emotional. My mother was almost a stranger to me. She smelled nice, sort of warm and sweet, and had the softest skin as she placed her arms around me to hug me close. Her heartbeat was fast, and we were both breathing as if we had just run a marathon.

I could not take my eyes off her. Actually, there seemed to be two of her and two of my aunt. My eyes were so watery all the time, and that band around my throat was back. It seemed to get so tight that my chest was swelling up, and I was afraid it might burst.

My mother told me how much she loved me and how happy she was to see me, but in my despair I don't think that is what I felt. I thought that since she had two other children, she did not need a third. So it was probably better that I was placed here. I was turning into a very angry girl.

They had brought me a wonderful gift. I had turned seven not long ago, so this was a bonus for me. It was the most stunning dress I had ever seen. It was made of shantung silk with delicate lilac-colored orchids printed on it. It had puffy short sleeves, a pretty collar, and a sash belt that tied in a bow at the back, a flared skirt with three petticoats. One of them even had a tube to blow it up, so that the skirt looked fuller.

I was so in love with that dress. I could not wait to put it on and show them. Matron said no, however, and told me that I could show them next time they came for a visit. Mommy said that now I knew they would come back for a visit, and that we all had something to look forward to.

I told my best friend about the dress and bragged about how lucky I was. Many of the kids had seen me holding the dress up in front of me, as visits were not private. I entered the home after my mommy and aunt left it had been a stressful visit for all of us. Matron confronted me.

She held out her hand for my dress and said that she would place it with my other clothes in the linen room. I begged her to let me keep it for a while, but she refused. I cried so much that day; it was as if someone had torn my heart out. But rules were rules, and none of the kids got to keep anything in the dormitories.

Come Sunday I asked Matron if I could wear my beautiful dress. She said she had no idea what I was talking about, and that I must be mistaken about the dress. She mumbled something about kids with overactive imaginations. At first I was confused and just stood there looking at her, until I realized that she was actually serious.

I started crying and screamed that she was a liar and that I wanted my dress. The other staff looked on in pity but dared not say a word. Just then I saw Matron's favorite girl prancing around in my beautiful dress.

I gasped and cried out, "That is my dress. Why are you wearing it?" The girl looked at me innocently and said, "No, it's not. Matron gave it to me."

I looked at Matron. Her face was expressionless. She would not look at me and turned as if to go.

I was so upset; I seemed to have no control over myself. I just screamed and screamed, and they dragged me away and put me in the Well.

The Well

As you walked through the front entrance of the home, you immediately noticed the smell of hospital cleanliness. Directly to the left of the door was a set of stairs that led down to the lower dormitories.

I was always so afraid of that part of the building. The tiles were a light grey color, and if there were windows to allow the light in, I saw no evidence of them. It looked like it was dim in there, and it made me uneasy. I never went down there voluntarily.

At the bottom of the stairs was a sharp right turn, which led past the linen rooms and an office situated to the left. On the right was another set of stairs. These stairs led to the Well. In hindsight, the place reminded me of a cellar.

As I was led down the stairs, not one word was spoken. All I could hear were my dry sobs for my darling dress. Those stairs filled my nightmares for many years thereafter and I became extremely claustrophobic.

I felt Matron's hand move to my back. I thought she was going to comfort me and tell me it had all been a mistake, but the next thing I knew, a door had been flung open and she pushed me forward. Before I could turn around, the solid wooden door slammed shut behind me.

Darkness enveloped me, and I let out a cry that to my own ears sounded like a wounded animal's. As my eyes adjusted, I saw a faint light coming from what looked like a slit in the top of the wall.

I whimpered as I moved around gingerly, hoping not to come up against some monster that they kept down there. As I made out the shape of a bed I made a beeline for it and lay down. I must have cried myself to sleep. A noise woke me up, and a staff member brought me some dinner. She also gave me some pajamas and told me that I had to spend the night there until the devil in me was gone.

"Oh God, Oh God." I must have said those words a million times that night. I just never could understand what I had done wrong. As the night progressed, I stayed wide-awake because of the sleep I had had earlier. I then began to notice the smell. It was musty, like damp washing that had been left to go moldy.

It was so dark now, and there was no light in the Well for me to switch on. I was cold and shivered so much my tummy ached. My legs felt weak, and I trembled from the fear that was welling up inside me.

How was it possible that this was all there was? How could I come into this world just to be tortured and put down? Was this how everyone else felt, or was it exclusive to a few people that were unworthy of God's grace? I berated myself for having felt so strongly about the dress. I wondered if God thought I loved the dress more than him.

Emotionally, I was on a downward spiral. The world seemed to be against me, and even my only friend was worried about me. I was only seven years old, but it felt as if I had been living for hundreds of years. I felt forsaken by everyone. I spent two days in that hellhole, and during my stay in that orphanage I was interned in the Well three more times.

A number of children spent time in there, and I can tell you it almost broke me.

The school we went to was almost a mile away from the home, and we walked to it in formation, each child holding another child's hand.

We passed a candy shop that had closed down, and one day one of the kids found a broken window. After that we would take turns running across the road and fill our schoolbags with the lollipops that had been left behind. There was no staff member with us, so we all had plenty of fun getting up to mischief.

One day I got so carried away looking around the shop, that when I glanced up I realized the other kids had already left and were getting too far ahead of me. Without thinking I ran out into the road, and a VW was heading straight at me.

I heard the squeal of brakes, felt a slight hurtful bump on my hip, and then a sharp pain as the car ran over my foot. I sat there in a daze until a very nice lady picked me up and put me in the back of the car. She kept saying she was sorry, as if it were her fault. I began to feel rather upset myself, until I too was crying.

She drove me to the home, where a doctor who thought I looked fine inspected me. I got into severe trouble because of the candy shop. Someone had seen me in it and reported it to the Matron.

I never told Matron about the other kids being in there, and neither did the witness. However, that place was boarded up pretty quickly. I think that precipitated my next trip to the Well, and believe me; it was no less frightening than the time before.

Actually it was worse, because now I knew I had done something wrong and was waiting for the wrath of God to settle on my shoulders.

One day a number of us were given the punishment of not being able to watch the movie that night. We found to our delight that if we lay on our stomachs, we could just see into the dining room where the movie was being shown. We had to be very quiet, but because we were in the upstairs dorms, we could not be detected from the dining room door.

Although we did not hear the words spoken, we heard the music, so we made believe that it was a silent movie like in the twenties. We never got found out and continued to do it whenever we were punished. It felt good to have power over Matron, and it gave us something to smile about secretively when she was around. I think it really made her mad that we could still have a laugh in that place.

I continued just to exist, barely understanding one day from the next. Wishing someone would find out about me and come and whisk me away from this place of pain and misery. I cannot talk for the other children, but I know one thing: in all my life since then, I have never felt so much sadness and heard so many silent sobs in a room filled with children.

My eighth birthday came and went without any sign of my mother. I had sort of come to terms with being in the home, and although I still found it extremely depressing, I had adjusted to the way of life. A nice new staff member helped. Her name was Auntie J. She talked to us in such kind tones and smiled a lot. All of us girls really took to her, and she sometimes would let us go with her to the office.

I had found a really nasty boil on my knee, and it seemed to be growing by the day. Auntie J wanted to put plaster on it to draw the infection out. Matron, however, thought we should squeeze it out. Auntie J told her that it would be too painful, and Matron reminded her that I was not a baby and that I would be just fine. I was hoisted up onto the table in the nursing station, and Matron prepared the boil for extraction.

Ah, it was a nasty-looking thing, and soon Matron was pressing away as if there were no tomorrow. I watched in horror as the boil grew bigger, and it became more painful with every push. The tears poured out of my eyes as if someone had opened a tap. Matron was turning quite red in the face and looked flustered.

Without warning, and almost in slow motion, the boil erupted like a huge volcano. Pus flew through the air like lava, splattering Matron's cheek and running down her chin. Through the tears of pain I laughed and laughed until I was almost hysterical. To this day I don't know why Matron didn't slap my face. Was it from her shock? Or was it because Auntie J was there and had been holding my hand the whole time?

Over the next year I got to know Auntie J very well. She was kind and considerate, and quick to help in any way she could. Sometimes she would let me stay with her in her little room near her office. It always smelled so nice and was as neat as a pin. She never showed any favoritism for any of the girls, and it is my belief that because of that everyone loved her. Everyone except Matron, that is, who did not seem to like anyone.

Auntie J always remembered our birthdays, special days, and everything we told her. She did not spend much time at the home, but that did not matter, because it gave us the opportunity to look forward to her visits.

That Christmas I spent with my mother and I don't remember a single thing about it. I think that is normal, and sometimes children forget large parts of their lives because it can be traumatic. This seems to have been the case with me. Sometimes events and days simply flowed into each other, and even got a little jumbled up in my mind. I have tried to be accurate with matching up events with my age. Still, there are things that just will not surface, no matter how I try.

There was days and even sometimes weeks that I lived with unbearable fear. Sometimes connected to the staff members in the home and sometimes an almost unbelievable fear of nuns. I would constantly be looking over my shoulder and checking under beds and in cupboards for something or someone.

I do know that life slowly became a little more bearable, and Auntie J had a lot do with it. It was hard to say good-bye to her when the time came to go on holiday. Little did I know that I would never see her again.

Food for Thought

Would my reactions have been different if I had known my own value? Would the home have been more bearable had I known that everything has to do with the choices we make, and any outcome is a consequence of those choices? I deeply believe that it would have, but for me that was not meant to be.

Had I known then what I know now, how would I have had the opportunity to help others today? Would I have become the strong and determined person I am now? How could I have discovered for myself through a life of conflict what made me feel good or bad, if I had remembered why I chose to come into this lifetime?

As each of us journeys in our personal growth of self-discovery, we make choices that at times might appear wrong to someone else. However, truth be known, there is no right or wrong, only perspective. What may appear wrong to you or me may not feel that way to someone else.

Each of us may appear unaware of what choices we made by deciding to come into this time-space reality. Therefore, it is not our place to sit in judgment of those who, to all intents and purposes, appear to be making the wrong choice.

Even though the people who were placed in charge of me seemed unkind, that does not mean they were without feelings. I hated them then, and for a long time I carried around with me all the baggage that came along with that hatred.

In my judgment of them, I found it hard to move forward. I could not love myself because I believed I was weak for accepting the life I thought I was forced to lead.

To judge other people is actually to judge you. You can only see wrong when your own insecurities become so evident to you, you need some form of distraction to take the focus off you. We need to remember to look only to ourselves and mind our own business.

I am in a place where I am free of the bonds of my religious upbringing. Free from the powerlessness that left me at the mercy of the limitations placed on me.

It is my deepest wish that by bringing you my story, you will be strengthened and inspired to see things from a different perspective.

Today there is power in knowledge. The more you know, the more powerful and unlimited you become. When dealing with any situation I find myself in, there is a moment of recognition about my options.

Realizing that it is all about choice and responsibility, and where these two important abilities come into play in my everyday life, gives me freedom and power over my reality. I am the creator, the writer, and the director of my story. Without question, this has allowed me to deal with my past and reach for the relief of letting go.

CHAPTER 4

From the Ground Up

"Children are resilient and can adapt to any situation." Linda Lang

WELL, THERE I WAS on a train, traveling to some faraway town that most people had never heard of. The reason they were sending me so far away was because, once again, my poor mother had tried to keep me with her. At the first chance she got, she had moved to a new home, taking me with her instead of dropping me back at the home. She had hoped we would not be found. As things turned out, we were.

A police officer came with the welfare caseworker while my mother was at work. They turned up at the door, and the poor housekeeper had no choice but to let them in. They dragged me down the stairs, and in front of everyone in the street they tried to shove me into their car. I was fighting like a cat and hanging on to the door for dear life. I am not sure if I actually expected someone to intervene on my behalf, but I do smile when I remember the look on the policeman's face as he took directions from the welfare woman. She barked one command after another as the poor guy struggled to get me into the car. His grip became firmer and suddenly he shoved me real hard. I opened my mouth and, with anger and pain in my heart, took a hearty bite of the policeman's leg.

After that it was a blur until I entered the gates to a place called the Place of Safety. Whose safety? I wondered. I was an angry and disillusioned girl, I can tell you, and even my mother said I was far too cheeky for my own good.

I could immediately see why this place was called that. There were bars on the windows and all the doors. I'm not sure if they were there to keep us in or keep everyone else out. I was immediately signed in, directed to my room, and told that my clothes would be brought up directly.

I sat on the bed for a minute to gain control of my emotions. I was over crying. I think I had cried so much in the previous years, my tears had dried up. Feeling calmer, I decided to take a walk around to familiarize myself with this new place. I walked towards the stairs and walked smack bang into a gate that had been locked.

I wrapped my hands around the gate and opened my mouth to scream, but then I closed it again and made the decision never to cry or lose control again. I returned to the bed and waited until they brought me my clothes. I remained there for three weeks.

The place was run like an army camp, exactly like they're depicted in movies. All of us kids walked around like automatons, as if we had been programed, which I supposed we had been. The girls' rooms were upstairs, locked behind gates of steel, as I said. The boys were downstairs with the same type of gates.

Our clothes had all been taken away and the staff supplied us with Government Issue clothes. All the girls wore exactly the same dresses and all the boys wore a shirt and shorts.

Clothes were handed out each day, even underwear and shoes. These people were nuts as far as I could see. I think they thought that if we had no clothes, we would not be able to run away. There were countless breakouts from that place, and God only knows what happened to those kids when they were caught. I never saw any of them again while I was there.

Visiting time for the kids in this place of safety was the most bizarre. Staff walked around keeping their eyes on all the visitors, who were sitting at tables and chairs dotted around the lawn. My mother came for a visit and it was all very uneasy.

The emotional upheaval we were both experiencing was unbelievable. I was almost nine years old now and I was very angry. I wanted my mother to report the behavior of the staff at this place, but she informed me that the welfare agency did not want to hear the story. After all, she said, they ran this place with the approval of the government.

To this day I wonder if that was just an excuse, even though I witnessed her tears and pain. A child cannot make heads or tails of the reactions of adults, and cannot predict how they will respond to certain situations. As young as I was, I made a decision that when I was grown up, I would never let anyone tell me what to do.

Welfare had decided to transfer me to an orphanage in a tiny town. This town was thousands of miles away from my hometown. It was all too much for my mother. They gave her permission to come see me off at the station. I held onto her hands through the train window as we both wept bitterly, even though I had sworn never to cry again.

The train whistle blew. As the train gradually pulled out of the station, both of us clung to each other's hands until we were torn apart by the speed of the train.

I saw my mother collapse onto the ground and a large group of people gathered around. I started howling like a dog for my mother. I think I almost fell out of the train in my agony to reach her.

The other girls who were with me held on to me. Was it out of concern for my feelings or the threat of the woman who watched us as if she was not even there? Did she feel anything? Was her heart tucked away somewhere in a dark little corner that kept her safe and protected from the agony of others?

I thought my mother had died and that I would never see her again. I would not have the chance to find out what had happened to her until we reached the new school.

I had been unceremoniously placed on the train with some other young children and a woman who assured us she had a gun and would use it if we tried to run away. Heaven only knows where she thought we would go at that age with no money, food, or clothes. Still she said to us, "If anyone tries to run away, I will shoot you." We all froze, and that day more of our innocence was taken from us, revealing to us an even more sinister way of life.

I had my first smoke on that train, and it was a Camel. It tasted so bad; I threw up out of the train door while it was going. This did not deter me, however, and I immediately had another one. At almost nine years old, there I was with the other girls, smoking in the train toilets. By the time we reached the orphanage in that tiny town, we were very experienced smokers indeed.

The woman seemed to have no interest in us while the train was in motion, but when it stopped she herded us back into the compartment like sheep and kept a good eye on us. The train journey took five days and five nights. We arrived at the station of our new home in the early hours of the sixth day.

The woman who escorted us was really a very nervous person, and she never seemed to look us in the eye. I wondered what she thought we would or could do. Very strange indeed. She immediately handed us over to the staff of the new orphanage and went on her not so merry way. I actually felt quite sorry for her.

She was also unable to let me know if my mother had died or not, as there were no mobile phones or the like in those days. Phones were still on party lines back then. A party line meant that an operator put through the call. Each home had a different ring and calls were never private. You could listen to other people's conversations just by picking up the phone.

CHAPTER 5

A Mountain to Climb

THERE SHE IS, THE little girl who sits at the window always crying and singing a little song that makes no sense to me. It is raining and she just stares ahead singing, "Sun, sun please come out, I will never be naughty again." My God, how did this child get to be so miserable? What about all the other kids here?

Most of the children were like me. They had been removed from their parents at an early age and placed in orphanages around the country. Talk about a lost generation. This issue was worldwide, it would seem.

My life became a burden to me as I absorbed all the sadness and misfortune that the hundreds of children in this orphanage felt. There were infants to kids as old as eighteen years old who had spent their whole lives there.

One of the young men that everyone loved and respected and who was voted most likely to succeed, had been there since he was about four years old. He had never been given the chance to connect with his parents.

All of these orphanages were thousands of miles from any cities or towns where the kids might have families. This young man finally left to start a life on his own, but he was afraid and lonely. He chose to take his own life.

The more I lived through these horrors, the more I became aware that something had to give and it was not going to be me.

I had a family out there somewhere that I had hardly seen, and it was my intention to get to know my siblings, whose faces I had all but forgotten. I still had not found out what had happened to my mother. I wanted a life. I was over being sad and distressed. I was over being treated like a second-class citizen. It was time for me to decide where all this misery was going to lead me, and it was not going to be straight to hell like all the grown-ups kept telling me. How could my life have made me so unworthy that I needed to burn in the fires of hell?

I have always been afraid of hurting and disappointing other people, and even when I was a child, my mother used to say I was too kind and too giving. Apparently when I was sent to buy bread or meat at the shops, I would return home with a long line of the neighborhood kids behind me all eating lollies from the leftover change. I also was sometimes minus my clothes, except my panties. Even my shoes might be missing. When my mother asked for an explanation, I would inform her that some of the other kids did not have shoes or a dress or whatever, so I gave them mine. I had no idea why I did this, and I am not even sure if anyone taught me to give to others. I believe that deep down inside everyone is a good person until disillusionment, confusion, and anger get the better of us, and we stray from our connection with God Source.

Now, however, I was a very different angry and disillusioned girl. I was in my third orphanage since I had been taken from my family. I was sick and tired of being pushed around from place to place. I was tired of being teased without mercy and totally fed up with this God who was doing nothing to help my situation at all.

This place was enormous, and the children were divided into different hostels according to age and gender. Children from newborns to six years old were placed together in one large hostel. The whole place was run as a self-sufficient home, with a couple as the house parents of each hostel. We had a community kitchen where all the food was prepared and then delivered to each hostel twice a day on weekdays and three times a day on weekends.

Summers were warm and pleasant, and winters were very cold with snow. I had never seen snow and was really looking forward to my first time. The orphanage was situated at the foot of mountains, and in the spring the foothills were covered in the most beautiful array of wildflowers. They spread all around as far as the eye could see and looked like a colorful carpet.

The town was very small, and one shop supplied everything from hairdressing, shoes, and groceries, to bed sheets and needles. The only thing they did not sell was a coffin. The shop next door tended this to. There were many churches, one post office, and a town hall.

I heard that when visitors came to stay at the only hotel at wintertime, nothing but icicles came out of the taps. We had a police station and one fuel station. This place was to be my home for the next seven years.

Each hostel had six bedrooms with four kids in each room. The rooms started from the youngest to the oldest. The prefects were in the last bedroom and they had the run of the place.

Some kids became their pets by doing little chores for them, but I was totally over running around like someone else's slave, and I swore to myself that things would be different now. I was going to be strong no matter what, and I would never again show fear of anyone even if I were terrified to death of him or her.

My first night there I wet the bed, even though I had no water a few hours before bedtime and used the toilet before I went to sleep. I was told in no uncertain terms that this would not be tolerated, and that if I ever wet the bed again, I would never be allowed to see my family.

From that day forward I never again wet the bed. I remained awake every night until just before dawn, when I would run to the toilet just at five o'clock. I would return to bed to sleep for one hour before it was time to get up. If you know what it is like to be deprived of sleep for long periods of time, you will no doubt understand that I lived a life of utter hell.

I was always so tired, I could hardly think straight at school. It took every effort I could muster to remain alert during the day. I learnt to take little naps during lunch break, and on weekends I would sleep in an old bus that was in the park. To this day I still struggle to sleep at night, and sometimes find myself awake until the early hours of the morning.

I was the kind of child that always asked questions, and I was constantly instructed to believe what I was told and not argue about issues I had no understanding of. Too right that I didn't understand how I was given the right to choose and then told to do as I was ordered or suffer the consequences.

What kind of choice is that? I attended as many different churches as I could, always seeking for something. I was not quite sure what, but I knew I would know when I found it. This separation and loneliness did not sit well with me. I could feel there was more to this life than I was being told and I had to find what it was.

I started to notice how I felt about certain things. If I felt bad I would go do something constructive to take my mind off what I was feeling; if I felt good I would just sit there and enjoy the moment.

That was how I started to build a wall around me, which made it easier for me to hear only what I wanted to and block out the rest. Some of the kids might have thought I was cold and unfeeling, but it didn't matter to me. Unkind words washed off me and I didn't give two hoots about what others thought of me.

I cannot tell you how much more powerful I felt when I realized that if I just ignored the kids when they were being mean, I could focus my attention on a better feeling thought and have more control over how I reacted to the mean words being uttered. So I would make believe that I was really tough and not be affected by what was happening around me. Kids started to leave me alone, picking on someone else instead.

With my newfound independence and power, I made a friend. That friendship lasted for all the years that I was there. She was a lovely person, and I liked the fact that she never spoke badly about anyone. She just got on with her life as best she could.

I started to laugh a little, not because I was happy, but because I wanted to feel happy. Sometimes I got a little hysterical and almost started crying. I liked the way my mouth turned up at the corners when I smiled. I had always thought my mouth looked like an upside-down moon when I was a child, and now I know why. I hardly ever laughed as a child, and neither did a lot of kids in the orphanage.

I have condensed the story of my life down to only a few short episodes, so that you can see how gradually I began to discover my power in a limited way. That brought me to a better place in my life.

I also found myself more in tune with the boys because I loved sports and was very much a tomboy. We rode donkeys and talked about sports. I never played many sports myself, since rugby and soccer was limited to boys only in those days. But boy, I was the best and most loyal spectator.

During my ninth year I was sent to a foster home for the Christmas holidays. I was very intimidated, as they were well off and lived in the sort of house I had only ever seen in the movies. When I first arrived at their home, a cat was sitting on the pillar of the gate. It was so big I thought it was an ornament, and almost freaked out when the thing moved and jumped off the wall.

They had a daughter about my age, and maybe that was why I was there: to keep the poor little rich girl happy. I really disliked the fact that I was forced to go. It seemed like they felt sorry for me, and I did not need their pity. I could have been wrong—who knows? When you come from a place like the orphanage, it felt hard to be magnanimous and it was easy to feel sorry for myself.

I remember we went to a farm where the people had cows and left their milk at the gate for the grocer to pick up for the people in town. I also vaguely remember a birthday party in an enormous barn, but then there is a large blank with no more memories at all about that holiday.

The Lord Gives and the Lord Takes Away

Grade three was the year when I learnt about unconditional love. Of course I was unaware of this kind of love, as my life so far had taught me only disempowerment. I had learnt that the happiness of others was of paramount concern, and it was always my responsibility to make sure I did everything in my power to please those around me in order for them to love me.

The unconditional love came in the form of my teacher. She was a spinster who lived in a little flat in town that was so small, more than two people in it at a time was a crowd.

She adored working with us kids and always paid more attention to the things we excelled at rather than what we had more difficulty with. She smiled often and had a voice so gentle, it felt like a cool summer breeze. If you were having a bad day, she could lift your spirits merely with her smile and gentle touch.

Her form of teaching encouraged all of us to be proud of everything we did and also be proud of whom we were. She let us know in no uncertain terms that no one person was better than another.

When she explained something to you, she would put emphasis on the words that were most important, making it easy to understand what she was trying to teach. If you still did not understand, she would never embarrass you in front of the other kids, but approach your desk when she was doing the rounds in the classroom in order to give individual help.

I experienced my first real rush of emotion towards this wonderful being, emotions that had been locked away for years. I visited her apartment briefly once, while helping her transfer some stationery to the school. She became my light in the darkness and my strength at school.

One day she gave me a "tickey." This was currency at that time and was equivalent to two and a half cents. It was a lot of money in those days. I cherished that tickey for many months. Miss B., as I called her, gave so much of herself to everyone she met, without needing them to be anything or anyone but who they were.

In the one year that she was my teacher, she never said an unkind word or criticized anyone for being different or nonconforming. The love she gave was the love I have searched for all my life ever since.

One night just before the Christmas holidays, a cloud settled over my life. Daybreak came, and although the sun shone and the sky appeared blue, darkness permeated everything. The sun went black, the sky turned to ink, and the birds stopped singing. My heart froze in my chest, and that horrible band that always tightened around my throat was back, trying to choke the life out of me.

We went to school, and a teacher came into our classroom. She stood in front of the class and waited for silence, which came pretty quickly. We were not used to seeing someone else at Miss B.'s desk and we were curious.

Her announcement came: "Last night Miss B. died, so she will never be back to teach this class again."

Gasps of horror could be heard throughout the class, and then sobs of despair filled the room. Even the walls and desks seemed to be crying as the deep loss every one of us felt permeated the classroom.

"That will be enough of that," the teacher said. "We have to move on. Your new teacher that will take your class for the rest of the year will be in shortly." She turned and walked out the door without another word.

There were no kind words or concern for those of us who had loved Miss B. which we all did; nothing else just those words. I sobbed for my lovely lady who had put her arms around me and made me feel safe while I was with her. I could not understand what it all meant, as I had not yet been confronted with death.

Later that day we were told that we would attend her funeral on Saturday and that we had to wear our Sunday best. We were to meet at the community hall and from there we would walk to the graveyard. We were not allowed to attend the service first.

So many people cried, and I had never realized how many people knew her. It was only a very small town, and I could not for the life of me see where all these people came from. It was as if heaven and earth had come together to mourn the departure of an angel.

The priest gave the eulogy, and then we sang "Nearer My God to Thee" and her favorite song, "The Lord Is my Shepherd." As her coffin was being lowered, I stepped up to the grave and threw the tickey that she gave me into the hole. The priest was saying the Lord gives and the Lord takes away, and I became so angry with him for taking away the only person to show me love. How dare he. When was this two, or were they three, in one going to stop making my life on earth a living hell?

I never got over the death of my teacher and the awful sound of sand hitting her coffin. I had terrible nightmares about her waking up underground and trying to claw her way back out. How could they be sure she was dead?

God, it was so horrible for a child to witness something like that without having the least understanding of what it meant to be dead. As they say, however, children are resilient, and I just accepted that she was never coming back. I got on with the life I had and kept her close to my heart in my memories.

Still, school was never the same again without her. My life was never the same again, and as the shutter came down over my heart, I swore I would never again love another. I believed that if I did not conform those that I loved would be taken away from me as punishment

Secretly I hated this God that everyone was so afraid of, and I swore to take my revenge on him one day. I was not sure how, but I was going to expose him for the fraud he was. Anyone who hid from plain view had to have a secret, and by Jove I would find out what it was, if it took the rest of my life to do so.

Two teachers at the school had an awful reputation for cruelty towards the kids. They were a husband and wife team, and it was said they never smiled or said a kind word to anyone. The male teacher was accused of holding a child by the feet and banging his head on the ground. This story was recounted throughout the school, but not one person at that school, man, woman, or child, had actually seen it happen.

What no one knew was that I had found out his or her secret. When they were alone together, they smiled all the time and even kissed each other. When they saw me, they once again appeared to be stern and lost their smiles. I thought at the time that they did not want God to know they loved each other, because then he would get jealous and take them away from each other.

I was positive they had the real secret about God, and as long as they did not smile at us kids, he would never know how they felt about each other and their students. I did know one thing, though. They had no children of their own and so they had learnt how to keep themselves safe from God's prying eyes and jealous nature.

I once heard someone say that having children was the worst kind of punishment a parent could receive from God, because then he had a really great way of keeping them in line. If they did not listen and obey him, he would take that child away from them.

These smart teachers had it all worked out, and I was going to use this same secret as I grew up. I would never share it with anyone, because the only time it worked was when you found out for yourself.

What Is the Truth?

> *Soon the child's clear eye is clouded over by ideas and opinions, preconceptions and abstractions. Simple free being becomes encrusted with the burdensome armor of the ego. Not until years later does an instinct come that a vital sense of mystery has been withdrawn. The sun glints through the pines, and the heart is pierced in a moment of beauty and strange pain, like a memory of paradise. After that day . . . we become seekers. Peter Matthiessen*

I was always swapping churches. I started off with the Methodist, went to the Anglican and the protestant, and then the Reformed Church, and so it continued. None of them brought me peace or closer to God. The orphanage was a very religious place, and we were forced to attend religious services twice every Sunday. There were no exceptions to the rule, and if you had no denomination, they would appoint one for you.

People seemed so nice at church, but I soon found out to my dismay that those same people were not so nice away from church. It seemed to me that there were places that you could hide from God. I just had to find them.

Was it okay to show fear of God only when you were at church? Maybe he could not see us unless we were in his house. Maybe that was why the adults changed when they were in their own homes.

All that I learnt made me feel inadequate, unworthy, and yet even more confused. There was a song that we sang in Sunday school that said I was a child of God's care, yet with the next breath it told me that I was oh so unworthy.

How was this possible, and who could hold the balance of power to such an extent? I had to discover for myself where I fitted into the scheme of things. If I was the child of this entity, how come I had no choice, no power over my life, and I was unworthy of his consideration?

I needed to know my truth, not anyone else's. Moving from one church to another brought me no closer to my truth, it was a little like my home at that time, nonexistent. I was like a small grafted tree trying to put down some roots, but I had no rootstock to take hold in.

There were too many variations, as far as I could see. Kids talked among themselves, and we had so many different interpretations of what we all heard and read.

We were in awe and fear at one and the same time. Life can be confusing when you are an adult, but it is so much more bewildering when you are a child.

Sometimes two adults give you totally different interpretations of what they perceive to be right or wrong, a truth or a lie. Some people come from a place of fear; others simply repeat what they have heard. Some cling to obsessions while others form their lives around love.

As a child you absorb everything, no matter how jumbled up it is. As you get older, your interpretations of all that you absorbed become your belief system.

Many people write books about their perspectives of their personal journeys, and that may be their truths. However, when you come from a place where I have been, a lot of what people talk about makes no sense at all.

When you feel low and unhappy, you just want those who think they have all the answers to go away and fall into a sinkhole.

For those of us who have just been looking, becoming more confused and more separated due to our enquiring natures, it is nice to know we are not alone or strange in our meanderings through life. Sometimes an old memory can jolt us out of our self-limiting beliefs, opening us up to a new and improved perspective of who we are and where we want to be in relationship to our lives and the people in those lives.

As a child though, I had no perspective other than the one I was being forced into. No one wanted to answer my questions, and when I did ask, I was always on the wrong side of the rules. I loved to sing and I loved the tunes of the hymns, but there was no conviction in my voice when I sang the words.

It was as if someone was reading the words to me for the first time and I had no idea what they meant. So how could I feel them? Sometimes I would sing the words and then I would feel a withdrawal so intense, I would change the words to the song using the same melody and then sing the new sad and disempowering song.

I spent many hours at night talking to Jesus, asking for help and guidance. Most of those times I came away feeling so disappointed and frustrated, because there seemed to be no answer.

It took many years of pushing for what I wanted before I actually got an answer. Often we don't realize that the harder we try to find answers, the more they elude us. The day I gave up trying was the day I found my truth.

CHAPTER 6

Upstream

A NEW GIRL ARRIVED. She was with her mother and they were walking a little Chihuahua with a beautiful studded collar. The little girl and her mother were so well dressed. They were talking in subdued voices. Well, mostly the mother was talking and her daughter was listening. They looked so out of place at the orphanage. They were smiling, and the little girl seemed so serene.

The mother left and the girl remained behind without the dog. She never recovered from being left behind. One morning after a large downpour of rain, we saw her walking in the gutter, picking up worms and eating them. We were shocked, as she had seemed such a gentle soul, although very distant from everyone.

No one ever knew what became of her. One day she was there the next she was gone.

The orphanage was a very active place with children coming and going all the time. We had children removed who were classified as crazy simply because they would not conform to the rules and regulations. Many children just could not hack the life that they were forced to lead in this children's home. It was amazing. The more misery I saw among the other kids, the more determined I was to get myself through it.

I realized there was almost always someone worse off than me. Now I started to be more aware of what was happening around me. Some children had no parents at all while some kids had lost their entire families to accidents. So even if I didn't have a mother, I still had two brothers out there somewhere and I was sure I would see them one day.

The little girl that sat at the window and cried every time it rained had had her entire family wiped out in an accident, and apparently she blamed herself. It seems she had been misbehaving just before they pulled over to the side of the road, and both of the cars her family were traveling in got hit by a truck. It was raining heavily at the time. How come no one ever told her she was not to blame?

I distinctly remember the words to one of the songs we sung, because they were so sad.

> I'm nobody's child, nobody's child.
> Just like a flower I'm growing wild.
> No mommy's kisses and no daddy's smiles.
> Nobody wants me. I'm nobody's child.

I never knew who wrote that song, but I knew it made us kids cry a lot. We would sit together in groups and sing these kinds of songs. We were abandoned and alone and lost in the darkness, which seemed to become darker as each day passed.

I just accepted what was going on. I felt so unworthy and was sure I did not deserve anything anyway, because I was so ungrateful. After all, I had a roof over my head and food in my belly. What more could I need? I decided that I had no time for God or anyone that was related to him. I thought that if I distanced myself from the fold, I would be able to make my way on my own. So I gave up God because he had given up on me.

Fragility of Life

I thought I had control of things. I was calm and ready to take on the world, so what happened next was very confusing. One moment I was on top of things; the next it was all too much for me.

Pieces of my life are just lost to me, and there are huge gaps that I can't remember. How do weeks or even months go missing? What happened to me during those missing times? These gaps persist to this day, but now they are of no consequence to me.

One morning as everyone was busy, the matron sent me on an errand. I was asked to go to the medicine cabinet and find some plaster for a kid. I found the medicine cabinet and a very large bottle of aspirin. I took handfuls of the pills and shoved them into my mouth, thinking how good it was going to be when I fell asleep in class and never woke up again.

If my mother were dead, would I get to see her without burning in the fires of eternal hell? I was still unsure whether my mother was dead or alive.

My God, I thought after I took the pills. I hadn't considered that now I was definitely going to hell, but it was too late and I could not tell the matron what I done.

During sewing class I started to throw up, and at the same time I was unable to keep my eyes open. The teacher thought I was unwell and sent me back to the orphanage with a friend. We had to walk, and it was the longest mile of my life.

My friend asked me what I had done, and I told her that I no longer wanted to live. She begged me to keep walking, because all I wanted to do was go to sleep on the road. Once we got back to the hostel, she informed the matron that I had taken the tablets.

When I woke up, I knew I was in hell. The orphanage was hell and I did not need to die to go there. I just had to find a new way of dealing with my issues. The other kids did. Why couldn't I?

I wondered if it would leak out what I had tried to do, but no one except the housemother and my friend seemed to know. I was relieved but not overly worried about it, as it was nothing unusual for this place.

Anyway, I did not care if the whole place found out. I was alive. That must mean I had some kind of reason to be here. I had no idea what it was, but I now knew I could make the choice to be strong or not. But why had I lived? Maybe the devil did not want me either.

I made up my mind from that day forward that I was going to be as hard as nails. No one was going to make me feel bad ever again. I would not cry ever again, and no matter what anyone said, I would only do the things that made me feel good.

This time I hoped that I could stand tall and walk tall and that I could stick to my guns.

A Reunion

I had been informed that my mother was alive and that she and my new father were going to pick me up for the holidays. I was terrified and yet over the moon with joy. From the age of eight, I had been under the impression she could be dead. I can't even explain to you the feelings of elation mingled with fear and confusion that coursed through my body. My heart seemed to be beating so fast, as if it was trying to escape.

Oh my God. I still had a mother and I was going to see her again after all this time. Two months short of my ninth birthday the scene at the train station had played out so it had been two years and 3 months since I had seen or heard from my mother, with only that memory still fresh in my mind.

It was June, and it was freezing cold and snowing. I was wearing shorts and a T-shirt and jumping on a trampoline covered in snow when my mother and two men arrived to pick me up for the holidays. My mother looked mortified by what she saw and was shaking her head at me with just a hint of a smile on her lips.

My mother had dyed her hair blonde (the last time I saw her she had dark brown hair) and she was with this really gorgeous-looking young man. She did not even get out of the car, but just sat there clutching what looked like a baby. She called my name and waved her hand in my direction. The other man in the driver's seat also remained in the car. The handsome young man extracted himself from the passenger seat in the front and greeted me with a beautiful smile. He introduced himself to me.

"Hi I am your step father and we have come to fetch you for the holidays. Shall we go and pick up your clothes from the hostel?"

We drove down to the hostel to fetch my suitcase. I felt so alone, and nervous even though my new father seemed so nice and smiled a lot.

The friend's car was white. My mother looked beautiful, and she had my little sister with her. She was only a baby, maybe six months old. The two men sat in the front and I was in the back of the car with my mother and my little sister.

It was wonderful. I talked nonstop and kept saying how happy I was that she was alive. I could not take my hands off her. She smelled so warm and nice, sort of musky and soft. Her skin felt like velvet to me, and I just wanted to stroke it all the time. My heart was brimming over with all the pent-up love of the years we had been separated. I was devouring her with my eyes just in case I woke up and found it had all been a dream.

As we drove out of the gates, warm tears started to well up in my eyes. I swallowed hard and remembered my promise to myself. I was not weak and simpering anymore. I was strong and determined now.

We were coming to a railroad crossing. A train was coming, and I expected we would have to wait at the crossing for the train to go past first. I was horrified that my new stepfather and his friend decided they wanted to race against the train to see who made it over the crossing first. It was the most frightening experience, as we only barely made it over, the car swinging to the side and just out of reach of the train. I was terrified, my mother seemed mortified, and my sister was crying, even though she did not know what had just happened. The men were laughing in the front. I couldn't see the joke.

For many years afterwards crossing train tracks left me paralyzed with fear, whether I was in a car or walking. If the bell warnings started when I was halfway across, I had to force myself to continue instead of just sitting down right where I was because of my fear.

The countryside was so beautiful and everything seemed to be going well, when suddenly the car developed a strange sound. My stepfather's friend suggested we should stop at the next town to see what was wrong. When we got there, the mechanic informed us that the car was in a bad way and it would take a few days to repair.

There was no money for a hotel, as they were on a budget, so we had to sleep in the car. It was not a very big car, so we were all cramped up together.

During the night I felt someone's hands on me. It was my stepfather's friend, touching me inappropriately. I cried out and crawled between my mother and my sister. My mother wrapped her arms around both of us, and I went to sleep.

In the morning I told her what had happened. She was furious. After she'd had words with my stepfather, they agreed to find another way for my mother, sister, and me to travel.

My stepfather placed us on a bus of schoolchildren who were on their way home from boarding school for the holidays. It was a tiring but pleasant tip. The kids sang a lot of the way, and I got to make some new friends. I did not tell them that I was from an orphanage. I was sure they would be unfriendly then, the way the other kids who lived in the same town as we did were. Those kids thought they were too good for the likes of us.

We reached my mother's home, and my stepfather arrived a few days later minus his friend. Thank goodness.

My parents lived near a drive-in theatre in a very small but neat apartment so I got to go to the movies often. We would sit on the embankment that faced the screen and watch silent movies, although we did get to hear the music that came from the outdoor theatre.

The neighbors had rabbits. I was so grateful I didn't find out until much later that they actually bred the rabbits for food. I loved animals a lot more than I did humans and would have been most upset.

The young men in the apartment next door had a band and loved to sing. I thought they had beautiful voices, but their singing seemed to drive my stepfather crazy. Music soothed and uplifted me, and when I closed my eyes I was in a paradise that was unreachable to everyone but me.

Music was my connection to something that allowed me to escape the pressures of life. When I was singing or there was music around me, everything else ceased to exist. Today I say that music is food for my soul. I come alive when I sing, and feel connected to all that I am and all that I am becoming.

I had the opportunity to get to know my baby sister and was so in love with her. She had the most beautiful eyes and smile that I had ever seen. I played with her all the time and never wanted to leave her side.

My brothers were not there. The one who had been taken away at the same time as I was had been placed in a school for boys. Later we found out that the two men who ran that place were pedophiles, and they had abused many of the boys.

According to my mother my youngest brother had died. She said he had suffocated while he slept. *Thanks again, God,* I thought. I had not even had the chance to meet him. I also had another sister, but she was living with her father and his parents.

Apparently his parents thought that my mother was not of good enough stock and breeding to marry their son. I wonder if they thought she was a horse.

There were so many places that we moved to, and sometimes it is difficult to remember which memory belongs with which apartment. I suppose that if my childhood had been less traumatic, I would have looked on it as an adventure. Amazing how circumstances influence our perception of what we see.

Anyway my mother seemed happy with my new stepfather and their baby. While I was there they moved again, but this time it was not to keep me there. I had agreed that it was in everyone's best interest that I went back to the orphanage when the holidays ended. Had I known what was to come I would have gone back that very same day.

The holiday from hell

I was eleven years old and at an age when wishes came true and beggars could ride and the whole world should have been my oyster. I had matured very quickly, as some girls do, and had become a woman with a child's mind. I was tall for my age and already had a lovely figure with well-developed breasts.

I was told I had beautiful legs that ran all the way up to my waist. This was a nice compliment for someone so young, yet also very unnerving. Vanity became my lifeline, and my ego became the wall that I could hide behind.

I was no longer allowed to join the young children at play, since—as was informed—God's curse was upon me. From now on I was unclean and an abomination in the eyes of God, as it was his punishment metered out to all women because of the evilness of Eve.

Even looking at a man according to matron would make me pregnant, which would send me straight to hell. I was told that once I was married and forced to comply with my wifely duties to procreate, I would understand, through the pain I would have to endure when giving birth, the full force of this curse.

As you probably understand by now, my relationship with a god of any kind was null and void. I refused to pray and only went to church because I was forced to. I must say that I knew some pretty nice people there who were young, and sometimes we all went on picnics together. That made it a little more bearable. The reason for this bit of information will become evident as I continue with my story.

I convinced myself that the weak and terrified side of me had to endure the worst situations. The other side of me was strong and unbendable. I had developed a split personality of sorts, and sometimes spoke about my weaker side in the third person.

I had not seen my biological father since I was four years old. This holiday with my mum was turning out to be many first time experiences for me. One such first time was when I met up with my father again. My mother had arranged for my father to meet me at a café that I was on my way to. I was so excited to see him again, and was almost hyperventilating as we walked along the shops and he bought me lollies.

We went to lunch and talked about everything under the sun, except the past. I avoided it since I knew that it would spoil this very precious time with my darling father. I had noticed that boys and men alike were impressed by me and I even got a wolf whistle or two. My father kept calling me his princess and touching my hand. He seemed so proud to be with me as he smiled indulgently at the attention I was getting.

He had a beautiful baritone voice that sounded like he was about to break into song, and his smile seemed to light up the place.

Time flew, and before I knew it was time to go home. I begged my mommy to let me go back to my dad's home for the rest of the day and also to let me spend the night. My world for now was complete and had taken a turn for the better. I wanted to savor each and every moment of it.

Mommy was hesitant, but then she agreed. I packed a change of clothes and my toiletries, and my father and I walked the short distance to where he and his new wife lived.

They had a beautiful high-rise apartment overlooking the ocean. The building was on the main road, which was lit up with so many lights and boasted some of the most spectacular buildings. There was even a fun park that was open all night long.

It was the most awesome place I had ever seen. They had a balcony, and it was wonderful to sit so high up above everything and watch the world go by. From up there the world was lit up like a Xmas tree. I had never seen so many lights before it was fantastic.

My stepmother was making dinner, and so my daddy and I sat outside and spoke about all the times we had missed out on. He started to sing a song called "Blue Velvet." He had the most wonderful voice I had ever heard.

He looked at me and said that the song reminded him of my mother, and that although he loved her, he knew he did not deserve her. He had by now consumed quite a few drinks, and so had my stepmother.

I knew my dad became somewhat angry when he drank too much, but I was in such a good-feeling place, I was sure I had nothing to worry about. Even after all the drinks he was still so happy to be with me, and he just kept telling me jokes and singing songs.

We had dinner out there on the balcony. Afterwards, I sat on their large bed listening to music while they continued to drink. I felt like the cat that had stolen the cream. I could not wipe the smile from my face as I snuggled down on the pillows to enjoy what had turned out to be the most fantastic day of my life. I must have fallen asleep, because my next memory is a nightmare.

Suddenly I was woken by a heavy weight on top of me. I could not breath I felt as if I was going to suffocate. I pushed against the weight and my hands encountered the naked skin of a body that was pressing down on top of me. I screamed, struggled and scrambled out of the bed, only to find that I too was naked. It was dark but I could see the silhouette of a man clearly naked it was my father. In horror I watched crying and trembling as my stepmother sat up she too was naked. My beautiful dream had turned into a nightmare. My head was reeling and I could feel the bile choking me as I sobbed uncontrollably, someone turned on the light as I frantically found my clothes and put them on.

My father kept saying sorry and crying, while his wife just stood there looking at us, as if she had no inkling of all the drama going on. My dad pleaded with me to stay and said he would call my mum to pick me up.

Instead, I ran out of the apartment, I don't remember getting into the lift or arriving on the ground floor. I just ran in the general direction of where I thought my mother lived even though it was late at night. I had no sense of direction, and to this day it amazes me that I found the place where my mother was living. I was in a terrible state as my mother tried to make heads or tails out of my blabbering words. As the words started to filter through about what had happened, my stepfather went into the most awful rage.

My next memory is of being back at my father's place and him running around naked, trying to avoid the belting that my stepfather was meting out. Why had he not dressed himself yet? As the vision floods back through my mind, the idiocy of a naked man running away from a beating seems like a scene from a very scary movie and I was the victim of a sickening plot.

What happened there and what I witnessed that night changed my life forever. I loved my father so much, without condition. He was my everything, and I had always been his princess.

Now however, although I still loved him unconditionally, he had broken my heart, taken my innocence, and destroyed my trust in him and anyone else. Words don't come easily to describe what I really felt at that time. Even though I have forgiven my father and put it all behind me, it has taken a tremendous amount of courage and self-love to be able to dredge up that piece of my past.

I never saw my father again after that. It was as if he had dropped off the face of the earth. I continued my holiday with my mother, stepfather and baby sister. No word of what had happened was ever uttered again; it was almost as if everyone decided that it had never happened. That is everyone but me.

My little sister was my solace during the remainder of my holiday. I would pour my heart out to her whenever we were together. I was not sure if she understood my pain, but she would look at me with such love, place her warm and tender little arms around my neck, and give me kisses.

This little darling was only about ten months old at the time. I wondered if the welfare agency would take her away as well. Was all the moving around my mother's way of making sure that it never happened to her again? I worried about my baby sister, so in my mind I created a story of love and security around her. Made her invisible to all who wished to harm her, especially welfare.

I remembered a time when her father, my stepfather, threatened my mother with a gun. He seemed very depressed at the time. It took my mother hours of begging and many tender words to get him to put the gun away. I grew up with a very strong dislike of guns. My sister was too young to understand but I lived with that vision for many years.

It is so easy for myself and others to judge this man, but unless we have walked in his shoes, it is best to keep an open mind and feel empathy for the life he created for himself. As the story unfolds this incident will make more sense to you the reader.

I returned to school and never spent another holiday with my parents until I was eighteen. I was told by the staff that my mother said I was too difficult to deal with. Could it be because she felt responsible for what happened with my biological father that she could no longer face me or look me in the eye?

In my eyes she was not to blame. Without being aware of it, we often create situations and circumstances in our lives that give us strength and character. I have and always will love her with all my heart. I feel sure she did the best she knew how under very difficult circumstances.

CHAPTER 7

Am I Responsible?

"I think, therefore I am." René Descartes

I CAN REMEMBER WHEN I was very young and not yet bitter and angry, how I used to sometimes sit alone in the park and weave the most beautiful fantasies about my life.

I had a fairy family and fairy brothers and sisters. We all loved one another, and gave, and shared, and helped each other. There were no tears, and I was unafraid of life and bogeymen.

When things got too much in the real world, I would retreat to this world of peace and harmony, until the rude awakening of my teacher's voice and her knuckles on my head. "Hello? Is anyone home? Are there any brains in this head? The way you daydream all the time, you will never amount to anything or anyone, you can be sure of that." She would remind me of that over and over.

Do teachers realize the damage they do to children when they fill children's head with their own debilitating and disempowering belief systems? I am not judging, only making an observation. After all, the teachers grew up hearing the same arguments and rationalization from the adults in their lives when they were children.

At such a young age, children can't make as much sense of things. Being trusting, they just accept what is going on and go with the flow. There is no point fighting against adults. They have all the power, so you better pay attention or you'll be nothing.

All the schools I attended were Christian based, so our upbringing was extremely strict and corporal punishment was very much the accepted thing.

As a young girl I would walk on my toes. It was my way of strengthening my calf muscles. Matron would complain about it to me and tell me to walk properly, so I tried to avoid her as much as possible. One day I was in the kitchen washing cups to make tea when I felt a sharp pain in the flesh behind my knees.

Matron had seen me standing on my toes again and she had sunk the tines of a fork into one of my legs. I screamed in pain as blood poured out of the wound.

"Go to the bathroom and clean up that mess," she said to me. "And let this be a lesson to you. Next time it will be a lot worse for you."

Lucky for me she didn't hit an artery. I could only wonder how she would have explained that one to the nurse.

I never walked on my toes in the hostel again or anywhere near Matron.

The staff that were our keepers had Carte blanch with the kids, and things went on that would make your skin crawl. However, giving a completely accurate account would be difficult. There is much I don't clearly remember, since children have this wonderful defense mechanism: they can just switch off and go into a world of imagination to get away from their fears.

Monday mornings we would attend scripture reading and listen to announcements that were made in the orphanage hall. All the kids would congregate in the hall, and the director would read from a very old Bible. It was the biggest Bible I had ever seen. It must have been about one and a half feet in length, one foot wide, and about six inches thick. It sat on a pulpit on the stage, and I heard it had been there since the place first opened.

One particular morning the staff seemed uneasy, and the director had a look on his face that I had never seen before. He was obviously furious and agitated as he strode towards the pulpit. There was a hush in the hall as never before, and all eyes were glued to him. He dropped his head down for a moment, and I swear he had been crying.

Suddenly he looked up and said, "There has been an abomination committed here in the house of the Lord."

At his words, electricity seemed to fly through the air, and it felt like everyone was holding their breath.

He wiped his hand over his eyes as if to clear his vision. We kids were too scared to look at each other. It is amazing how, because of the mindset that has been drummed into us, each and every child felt guilty. None of us had an inkling about what was going on or what had happened, but we seemed to have no control over our feelings of guilt.

We all waited with bated breath for what was to come, unsure about the announcement, though I was certain it was going to change everything. Slowly he raised his head, and I could see the emotion written all over his face. His eyes were red and his face was so flushed, as if he were using every ounce of control within him to talk.

He gripped the pulpit, leaned forward slowly, and said, "Someone took a knife last night and drove it into the Bible. He or she ripped every single page out completely."

To me it sounded like "someone took a knife and thrust it through the heart of our Lord." Children started crying as if this was what they had heard too. I just kept swallowing hard and telling myself, "You will not cry," not because of what had happened to the Bible but because of the tears that were being shed by the other kids.

I could not understand why they were so upset. I would soon find out what the consequences of those actions were, which once again changed the lives of every child in the orphanage.

The culprit disappeared from the orphanage, branded a crazy child, and the staff continued on with their lives as if nothing had happened. This seems to be a common trait among adults.

CHAPTER 8
Self-Discovery

OUR SCHOOL WAS SITUATED one mile from the orphanage, and a very nice gentleman and his wife ran the entire place. He was the founder and director of this school, and, man, could he play rugby.

I have never seen anyone in my entire life that could pass a ball the way he could. He would run ahead, always keeping his eye on the team member he intended to pass the ball to, and then he would throw himself forward while twisting at the same time, flying through the air as the ball left his hand and landed perfectly in the hands of the team member. We would cheer so loud for him. He won almost every single game because of his fantastic playing style and his sportsmanship.

Sporting day events were a big thing for us, because rugby is much loved in my country. Many people came from far and wide to join in the competition. Different grades and ages of boys played against each other, and the police and teachers from our schools and the town played against those of other towns.

Those of us from the orphanage were expected to walk around with a tin and ask for charity from the visiting teams' families. I could not bring myself to do that, so I hid among the parked cars, trying to look inconspicuous.

A young girl in one of the cars started talking to me, and we found we had a lot in common. She told me that her sister was a teacher and had just won a competition to fly around the world. She was so excited for her, but she knew she would be so lonely when her sister left, as they got on so well and shared most of their time together.

We talked about the places her sister might see and the things she might do. By the end of the day we had become firm friends and decided that we would write to each other every week. I was a little sad to say good-bye to her, but by then I was used to doing that to people I liked.

All permissions had been granted for leave for the Christmas holiday, train fares had been paid, and I was to spend the holidays with a foster family. I was so excited and close to tears, but I determined to keep the vow, to be strong and not cry.

I was a little uncertain as well. What happened if the welfare agency changed its minds and said I could not go? What if someone in the foster family died? What if the trip was cancelled? The more I thought, the more I worried.

Why do I keep doing this? I asked myself. Wasn't there another way in which I could enjoy where I was at that moment? I just kept singing to keep my mind off these debilitating thoughts. I was so afraid that if I kept thinking them, they would happen. How amazing—or maybe not—that even then I knew my own power, but was as yet unaware of the extent of that power.

I travelled by train to meet my foster family. The four days spent on the train were like a dream, and I met so many new and exciting people. There was a wonderful world out there that I had not yet experienced. All my dreams were coming true. I started singing songs that were no longer sad. The new songs were about freedom and power.

The foster family taught me many things, and one of the most important was that I didn't have to take anything lying down. I could get up and be proud of who I was. There was so much to live for, so much to see. I was young and had plenty of years ahead of me.

They gave me a family life, and I had the most fun. We listened to music and danced. We spent hours at the beach and I made some fantastic friends. They had a holiday house in the hills, and we spent some fantastic days swimming, horseback riding, picking berries, and getting to know each other. I was in heaven and I wanted more of the same.

Never at any time did they make me feel as if I was just a girl from an orphanage. I was treated like one of the family. I received so many Christmas presents, my cup overflowed with joy.

Then came the time to return to school. I was heartbroken but brave. Deep down inside, even though I was having a wonderful time, I knew that it was going to come to an end. But by then I had built up a resistance to being hurt.

I was determined to experience this joy again, so I behaved extraordinarily well, in the hopes that these people or someone else would be happy to share their home with me again.

I returned from that holiday a completely different person. I was fourteen and had discovered that I was as good as anyone else. Just because I had not grown up at home with parents did not mean I was inferior. I no longer had to humiliate myself with those ridiculous orphan collections and pretend to be someone that I was not.

Private schools or state schools, we are all one and the same. We are connected by something far more than our physical bodies. We are Source Energy (God Source). That in itself makes it impossible for anyone or anything to be better than or more important than another person.

I had been shown a life outside of the one I had become used to, and now I wanted that life all the time.

More Than What It Seems, or Perception

Many of us were shocked when we returned after the holidays to find that our director had left and there was a new man and his family in charge. This was directly related to what had happened to the Bible. Although no one spoke about it, that act of vandalism was always just beneath the surface, and many different circumstances and situations were created as a direct result of it. For a lot of us, life was to become even more confusing and degrading.

The new principal appeared to be very nice. He was a handsome and charming man, he smiled a lot, and he got on well with everyone, even the staff. He was friendly and had an air about him that said, trust me. I love you all and I will take care of you.

It was not long before some of us older girls discovered that what lay beyond that friendly exterior was a person with problems and issues that he wanted no one to know about.

He seemed to relish the power he wielded over us kids, and he was especially fond of taking a cane to us older girls. He hit me once so hard and often across my back with a cane that had been soaking in salt water, I had marks for years.

Gone was that little girl who gave away everything she had. I was growing up and learning to take care of me. I put up a wall of lead around me and buried my emotions and feelings in a place so deep, it took me a very long time to find them again.

I started paying more attention to what I looked like, paying less attention to what I was feeling inside my heart. The phrase "Think with your head, not with your heart" became my friend and protector.

I still wanted answers to all those questions that I had been asking. I wanted to understand why people did things that caused so much misery. Would knowing this make any difference, and could it affect me differently if I was more clued in to the antics of society? There was still so much for me to discover about life and what it all meant.

Everything in the Bible was taken literally, and we were taught that those of a different skin color were made by God to serve us with white skin. It was awful to have to hear and listen to that, and it made me feel as if I were responsible for all the misery that people of color had to suffer.

Most of the kitchen, laundry, and household staff had beautiful dark skin, sort of like hot chocolate. It was so smooth to the touch, and whenever I was outside I was covered in oil, butter, or something that could help me achieve that delicious dark skin.

They were gentle, kind, and so caring, and it was with these wonderful people I would seek comfort when things got too much. They would never berate, criticize, or insult me, as white staff members did whenever I made the effort to tell them my problems.

In my eyes these people, the true indigenous people of my land, had so much wisdom and spoke their truth with conviction and total honesty.

The pigmentation of one's skin is not a prerequisite to perfection or an indication of value. True value lies within the character and personality that one develops over the years. True value is assessed by the value you place on your fellow human beings and the respect you have for other people and yourself.

Sticks and Stones

One evening I was caught kissing a boy, or actually a young man by age standards. I was fourteen almost fifteen years old and oh so ready to fall in love. It was at the first dance party I was allowed to attend with the older girls. To me, it was just a moment of exuberance and newfound freedom. To the staff, you would have thought I had murdered someone. I was banished to the hostel and missed out on the rest of the evening's entertainment.

The next day I was called to the dining room and told that I had to be punished. One of the prefects, who disliked me immensely and was at least a few years older than me, had thought up a real doozy.

All the girls in the hostel had lined up on either side of a hall, making a tunnel for me to pass through. Each girl was armed with some kind of object, and as I walked down the hall I was belted by each one of the girls. The prefect had also told the girls to abuse me verbally, and so I was called every name under the sun. I was more upset about the bruises than I was about the names. As far as I was concerned, it took one to know one. I never really cared one bit what other people thought about me. I was a firm believer in the saying, "Sticks and stones may break my bones, but words can never harm me."

I felt sure I had outgrown the girls I was sharing a home with and that it was time for me to be placed in the older girls' hostel.

A Change of Pace

My request to be moved to the older girls' hostel was granted, and there I had a little more freedom and was encouraged to find the answers I was seeking.

The house parents and their son were very kind to the girls and even allowed us to sit with them in their private lounge and listen to stories on the radio. We were allowed to wear a small amount of makeup, as well as use nail polish. This may seem trivial to some, but to us it was *freedom*.

As I go through the revelations of my life with you, I notice the confusion of how at times I allowed myself to feel and at other times I didn't, and how that related to how I coped with the different situations in my life.

Locking away how I felt and ignoring emotional warnings created an outcome that left me feeling powerless and disoriented. On the other hand, opening myself up and allowing myself to heed the warnings that perpetually flowed through me gave me the power to deal with situations from a much more confident and stronger place.

I was unaware at the time of the importance of these differences, so I fluctuated between disempowerment and empowerment for most of my adolescence.

Now that I was in my teens and discovering things about myself that up until then had eluded me, I was also learning to be grateful for small moments of happiness. I was never over the moon with joy, but I had longer periods of peace than ever before, even when I was in difficult circumstances.

We still had to follow strict rules, but because of our age, we had a few more privileges. However, the indoctrination of religion and racism were very distasteful to me.

When I was fifteen, I had a visitor who would change many things in my life. Where as before I was just one of the girls I became a trusted and much respected older girl just by association with this beautiful young man who had come to visit. One morning while attending to my duties of cleaning my personal space in the communal bedroom, one of the other girls came in. She seemed flushed and uneasy as she blurted out, "There is the most handsome man at the door and he is asking for you. I don't think Matron will be happy that your boyfriend visits you here."

Perplexed I went to the door and there was my stepfather dressed to kill in biking leathers. There was no sign that he was related to me in any way. I laughed with glee as I informed the girls of our relationship, and was even more amused by their disbelief. It seemed that as a favor to my mother my stepfather had come a very long way to visit with me.

After I talked to the housemother, she agreed that he could take me out for a spin on his oh so awesome motorcycle. As I climbed on behind him, I could tell the other girls were green with envy. We took off like a jet at high speed on his 750cc Honda, with all the girls cheering and whistling.

We roared around town and stopped at the one store to buy things he thought I would appreciate. People looked at me in shock and horror, and over the next few months I became the talk of town for being so indecent as to sit pillion on a bike.

God would punish me for this indiscretion, and I would go straight to hell for so blatantly laughing in the face of his commandments and rules. I was a girl on a path of self-destruction, according to everyone, and there was no hope for me.

Had I gone too far this time or was this just the same misinformation for the sake of conformity? I must say the ride was so exhilarating the wind blowing my hair and my hands tightly holding on to the seat I felt a freedom that I had never experienced before.

I wanted to know more and so I read the Bible many times over, looking for answers that would prove them all wrong. But the more I read the Bible, the worse it sounded, even from my perspective.

I was tired of always asking questions and constantly being told to believe what I was told and not argue about issues that I didn't understand. I did not understand, for example, why we were given free choice, according to the Bible, and then told to do as we were ordered to or suffer the consequences. What kind of choice is that? Also how can something that felt so good be a bad thing? I needed to know more. Somewhere had to be someone that could explain it all to me so that it all made sense.

I continued to attend as many different churches as I could, always seeking something. I was not quite sure what I was looking for, but I knew I would know when I found it.

This life of separation and loneliness did not sit well with me. I could feel that there was more to life than I was being told and I had to find what it was.

I started paying more attention to people at church and even the teachers at my school. I listened closely when they were talking around me. I did not mean to be rude, but I found some of the answers to my questions. When people are unaware that someone is listening to their conversations, they open up more readily. And at my age, eavesdropping was not uncommon. It may have been impolite, but how else was I going to get the answers to the questions I was asking?

One of the unmarried teachers got pregnant, and this caused a huge commotion because the father was a married man and of some standing in the community. Since I was old enough to understand the rules of conformity and the unspoken rules of society, I wondered if this young woman would give her child away, as so many other mothers had before her.

Was this how my mother felt when her life fell apart? Would society have given her a better chance if she had been well off financially or if she had fought harder to keep her children? Somehow I don't think anything would have changed because of her self-limiting belief systems and the disempowering upbringing she had.

I was appalled at the unbelievable cruelty of society. It seemed to me that too many people thought they led such impeccable lives, and they then had the right to judge others. Other people's opinions appeared to have a powerful impact on those who were judged. They would hang their heads and look at the ground. Those who sat in judgment would thrive and walk around as if they owned the world.

In my view at that time, those people who judged others had secrets of their own that if they were discovered, would place them at the forefront of society's ridicule. Therefore, as long as they kept focusing on the supposed wrongdoing of other people, it would keep the eyes and ears of the world away from them.

Society's so-called pecking order baffled me. I could not understand how people allowed only a few people to have and wield so much power. These were the examples we had to follow as children. In our eyes, strength was not about kindness and compassion, but about judgment and being on top.

If you did not learn to be a leader, you were trampled all over. The kids soon learnt whom they could use to their own ends and how much they could push someone before that person broke.

Those of us who were "strong" became a force to be reckoned with. We knew how to make and break the rules, knowledge that I took with me after I left the orphanage.

CHAPTER 9

Flowers in Your Hair

*You are a child of the universe, no less than the sea and the sky; you
have the right to be here. And whether or not it is clear to you,
no doubt the universe is unfolding as it should. Desiderata*

THE SIXTIES WERE THE best. We had the Beatles, Elvis Presley, hippies and
the mods, and communal living. Free love for all was the saying. Flowers in
your hair, flowers everywhere. These were the words that rang out in song.

We made sandals out of wool, braided them, and decorated them with
flowers. People were smoking weed and tripping out of this world. I hadn't
got a piece of that action yet.

So much had changed since I was a child. Gone were the days when you
could not question the laws you did not understand. Gone were the days of
conformity and powerlessness.

As I became a teenager, the "Age of Aquarius" was being sung by all, and
people started looking at life from a more inspired perspective.

We had the hippies and the mods, which came from entirely different sides
of the spectrum. There was free love, but I wasn't sure what that actually

meant. There was Woodstock, the Doors, and Jimi Hendrix. Art changed and colors became psychedelic.

Nothing was as it had been before, and an electric excitement seemed to run through the air, affecting everyone in one way or another.

I don't think there has ever been another decade that offered so much opportunity and diversity, and so much encouragement to be different. People seemed excited and motivated to make changes, to make a difference, and to become a part of something that counted. It was as if the whole world had been asleep like Sleeping Beauty, until the kiss that brought life back into the very core of the Earth herself.

Hush, Not a Word

Teenagers, what can I tell you? Adolescence is when we become sure that we have all the answers, yet remain confused and angry when we ask the questions and the answers are not what we expected.

Talk about vanity. I suddenly realized my power over boys. Even though I was never promiscuous, I became what they called a tease in those days. I relished the power I seemed to hold over boys and men alike, and yet I never allowed them near me.

There was something in the recesses of my mind that I could not put my finger on. But I do know that at that time, it gave me endless pleasure to witness the discomfort of the male species around me.

Some girls accused male staff members of inappropriate behavior, but nothing was ever proven. Those were the days when everything was kept hush-hush, and no one spoke about abuse. If you said anything, you were accused of being delusional and in need of treatment. God knows none of us wanted to end up in an asylum for the so-called mentally disabled.

I remember a day when our new director summoned me to the office. I was wearing a yellow knit sweater that buttoned all the way up to my neck. I stood in front of him feeling very nervous. This was not the first time I had found myself in his office, and each time had been very painful.

"Unbutton your top now," he said.

I looked at him as if he were crazy. This was the first time he had ever said anything like that. "I will not," I said, and turned to walk away.

He barked out my surname and told me to stop.

The next thing I knew, I was receiving one of the worst canings of my life. He hit me all across my back, from just below my shoulders to my bottom, raising the cane high over his head before bringing down on me.

We all suffered similar abuse, and for most of us, life just went on. I felt emotionally abused, and was sometimes physically and mentally abused, but none of us had any recourse except to hold our tongues and get on with it.

A number of girls started putting on weight, their bodies becoming voluptuous. They were taken away. Some returned months later, slim again. Others were never seen again. There were some strange goings-on at that place, I can tell you.

Eventually one of our friends became involved in this secret world, she was sexually abused until she could take it no longer. We rebelled against the injustice of it all and ran away reporting to the police our fears and frustrations of what we had to endure. At the time they seemed to be very kind and understanding, and told us that they would investigate.

When we returned to the school, we could tell trouble was brewing. The school holidays were at hand and although all the other children had left for their respective destination my friend and myself remained behind at the orphanage with a staff member.

A few days before the school holidays were over and the other kids were due to return we were ordered to pack our bags and prepare ourselves for a journey to a new school.

The new headmaster that had been at the center of the abuse and violence would not be returning to the Orphanage, and the talk was that he had been replaced.

We had our revenge, but he made sure he gave us one last and terrible surprise. He had the last laugh by transferring us to another place that was called "A Reformatory School for Girls", and that convinced me that there was no justice in this world.

I was so embittered and angry at the system, it took many, many years for me to work through all the negative emotions I had accumulated over the years.

You see I had been led to believe I might be able to return to live with my mother, and now here I was back at the start again.

CHAPTER 10

One Step Forward, Two Steps Back

THREE MONTHS LATER, MY best friend and I were transferred to what we refer to as the Woman Prison. We were placed on a train, and during the three-day journey, we remained under strict security. We arrived at our new home in the early hours of the morning.

We were introduced to the houseparent and taken to our room. As we entered the room, the bell rang for all the girls to rise. There were fifteen to twenty girls in each room. The beds looked like the steel ones they have in the prison cells you see in movies.

My friend was assigned a bed two beds away from mine. We were told to unpack our personal belonging and that all private clothes would be taken away and placed in storage. Now where had I heard that before?

My friend moved the curtains aside to look outside and let out such a wail, even the girls that were half asleep sat up in alarm. As I look outside too, I realized there were bars on all the windows. The window looked out on an empty courtyard that appeared just as horrible as a jail. My friend started crying uncontrollably, and I had to hold on to every ounce of willpower not to join in.

Girls started moving around the room. Even though it was only 5.00am their day had just begun. They donned matching clothing. After removing their matching pajamas. Having made their beds, they left the room. One girl remained behind to sweep the room. None of the girls even spoke to us, although we did get some pretty strange looks.

I approached the girl who had remained behind; She was now on her hands and knees putting polish on the floor. She did not look up from her task as she told me that each girl was given chores, and these had to be done every morning before breakfast. She had to sweep and polish the floor. Once the polish was dry, she scrubbed the polish off with scouring wool and then returned to shine the floor. After that she would need to sweep again to make sure the floor was dust free for inspection.

We left her to her chore. Even though we'd had little sleep the night before, we were told to get ready for school. After school, we would be told what our chores were. As we walked through the building, we saw girls on their hands and knees everywhere polishing huge expanses of floor, while others set the tables, cleaned windows and bathrooms, and still others were cleaning the outer courtyard. That looked like a losing battle, as it was a little windy and the dust just seemed to keep coming.

We had to give up our private clothes and were given what we called Government Issue clothes. They consisted of school uniforms and a dress that zipped up the front and looked exactly the same as everyone else's.

At precisely 6.30 am the bell rang for breakfast and there was no being late. You had to make sure all of your work was done and present yourself for breakfast promptly. There was a mess hall with sixteen girls at each table. The kitchen staff, some of which were residents of the home, had already placed food on the tables. We were introduced as the new girls and told to make it our business to find out what our duties were to be. Each hostel had a prefect, and we later found out that our prefect had killed her mother during a terrible fight. God, what the hell were we doing in this place? The worst things I had ever done was smoke cigarettes and kiss a boy.

This was crazy. We did not belong in a place like this. The more stories we heard about the other girls, the more convinced we were that there had been some mistake and we had been brought to the wrong place. I tried to talk to the matron about it; she told me to take it up with the authorities. When we asked whom that was, she said it was the head of the school. Was there any way we could see him we wanted to know? "Not on your life" was the answer. He did not have time to deal with our pathetic attempts to weasel our way out of what was probably a just punishment.

We were both sixteen years old and had been incarcerated in a young women's prison for having the courage to report what we believed was inhumane behavior toward children. So much for that policeman helping. Was there anyone we could trust? Were all adults bitter and mean to children? How long could we put up with the kind of girls we had been thrown together with? I was not placing judgment on them, as I had no idea what their circumstances were. Even if I did, it was not my place to judge.

This place was situated between two Training camps where soldiers were recruited and trained for the armed forces. There was no privacy in the hostels, and some of the older girls would sell their favors to the soldiers. This was done through the bars of the windows, and I am telling you this was no place for the innocent. You grew up very fast and learnt that it was each girl for herself in that place.

The bathrooms were the worst. Girls who had decided they'd changed into men because of the way they were treated behaved the way sexually starved men would around girls. If you think being raped by a woman could never be as humiliating as being raped by a man, think again. Some women are worse than men when it comes to sadism, and they could be downright cruel to the weaker girls.

I had been there for six months when I decided I could not stand it another day. The staff were vicious, and so were some of the girls. I had had a run-in with the headmaster of the school after I'd been locked up in a tiny room for over a week over some infraction. They would not let me out for a bath or shower, and after four days I was repelled by my own smell. I had a filthy bucket to use as my toilet, and I was not allowed contact with anyone.

As for the incident with the headmaster, I had the audacity to question their punishment for smoking. In a foul rage the headmaster slammed his fist straight into my face. I felt as if I had been hit by a freight train. My head exploded, and my eyes felt as if they were going to pop right out of my head. The pain was unbearable, and I reeled around his office like a drunk out of control. Blood filled my mouth, and I felt as if all my teeth were falling out. I was in such a state of shock I forgot to cry. Or was it because I had no tears left?

I was thrown back into that hellhole for another week to learn to keep my tongue. For heaven's sake, no wonder the girls were so hardened. How could they not be with this kind of treatment going on?

One of the girls was able to slip me a smoke that first night, and I swear it is the only thing that kept me from going insane. It was like the nectar of the gods and I savored every breath of it, inhaling it the way a drowning man sucks air into his lungs after being underwater for a long time.

It is amazing how much one appreciates the little things in life when confronted with situations that seem endlessly painful and debilitating. Smoking cigarettes helped me keep a level head because my belief system at that time said, "It takes away the stress and keeps me calm."

We create our belief systems out of whatever feels a little better than what we have just endured. In this way, We can face the real problem from a more empowered point of view.

CHAPTER 11

Breakout: From the Frying Pan into the Fire

THERE WERE WHISPERS THAT there was going to be a mass breakout, and it looked as if I had been invited. Something like that needed to be kept very quiet, because just as it is in most places like that, there are snitches that would do anything for a little freedom. Even tell on their companions and probably sell their mothers for five cents. It was hard to know whom to trust, and friendship meant nothing there.

All of the doors in the hostel were made of solid wood. They were bolted with padlocks to make sure they could never be opened without a key. The thickest one was in the bathroom, but that was the one the ringleaders had decided on. That was the door we were going to use to escape from the hellhole that was called home.

At 3.00 am, twenty-eight girls were gathered in the bathroom, all ready to take their chances on the outside. We were as nervous as hell, and I was shaking so badly, I thought I would throw up. Two of the strongest girls had pushed a steel bar through the padlock and had been working on it for a week. If any of the other girls had noticed, they knew better than to say anything.

That place was bad, and come hell or high water we were going to break out. Four of us now applied pressure to the bar, and as we balanced all of our weight on it, we could feel it starting to give.

We placed our arms around the bar and literally hung on, and suddenly the lock broke. In horror we watched as the padlock flew through the air in what seemed like slow motion. We all waited for it to hit the porcelain tiles and make the most awful noise.

We were frozen with fear, sure that all the planning and hard work was going to be in vain, and then a hand shot out of nowhere and caught the lock. Every mouth opened as if to cheer, but then we looked at each other. The breath whooshed out of twenty-eight pairs of lungs simultaneously, but you could hear a pin drop in that room.

Once outside, we crept silently towards the fence line. Now here was a challenge. You see the fences were seven feet high with barbed wire across the top, which leaned inwards at an angle. We had to scale the fence and push ourselves over the barbed wire without tearing ourselves to pieces.

Like pole-vaulters, we measured our distance. The idea was to vault up the fence as high as we could and then in one fluid motion, push ourselves over and out.

The high jumpers were bloody brilliant at it, and even I thought I had it licked. But my hand slipped just as I pushed up and my legs connected with the barbed wire. It tore into my legs like scissors into paper. Oh God, it was so sore, but I had no choice but to tear my legs free, or I would simply hang there until morning, when they would find me and probably beat me to death.

The guy that ran that place hated girls that tried to run away and always threatened to do some pretty awful things to them.

Just the thought of having another run-in with that guy was enough to dispel the pain and urge me on. I got up after falling seven feet down and ran straight into a sharp rock that was jutting out of the ground. I went down like a ton of bricks and felt as if the bone in my knee had been shattered.

Suddenly the lights inside the building came on, and I scrambled for my life. I just got up with my friend beside me, and we ran as fast as we could until we came to a dark phone booth. My friend and I both scrambled into it and lay there until things quieted down.

We had all arranged to meet at the highway, where we would decide who grouped with whom. When we got there, I was amazed to see that almost all of us had made it. We broke up into three groups so that we would have a better chance of getting lifts. It was freezing at that time of the year, and even though we had jumpers on, we were turning blue from the cold.

It did not take long before a truck driver picked us up. We all bundled into the back with the stock he was carrying and I can tell you, it was a tight fit. We had to sit on our haunches so that all eight of us could be accommodated into the space allocated to us for the trip.

Before long we were all in severe pain from sitting in such cramped confinement. As soon as we got to the first garage, we jumped out, stretching our legs to get the blood flowing back into them. God it was painful, and to make matters worse, we didn't have even one cent to our name, so that we could get some coffee to warm us up.

One of the girls disappeared around the side of the truck and did not come back for a long while. When she returned, we all climbed into the bed of the truck again, and the driver promised to put us down in the nearest large city at dawn.

We arrived in the big city and split up again, this time into two groups. We decided it would be prudent to have even smaller groups now so that it would be easier to travel. The other three girls and I had only been hitching for about ten minutes when a young man offered us a lift.

He seemed very nice with lovely manners, and after about twenty minutes he pulled into a truck stop, took us to the café, and bought us all lunch. I suspect he knew we had run away, but he did not ask any questions. I am telling you, we were famished, and he knew it.

We tried not to scoff the food down too quickly. After our hunger had eased and we had finished our coffee, we piled back into the car and he took us to his house. For the sake of this story, I will call the man Bobby.

He appeared to live alone, but later we discovered that he shared the house with a mate. We found warm beds and bath towels that felt like down. The cupboards were full of food and the lounge was warm and cozy.

One of the girls decided that she wanted to move on. We tried to get her to stay, but then we gave up and she left. After she was gone, we discovered that my watch was gone too. Still, I didn't remember ever having had such a wonderful night's sleep, despite some commotion going on in another room.

The next day when I awoke, the men had already left for work. To show our appreciation, the other two girls and I cleaned the house and made dinner.

When Bobby came home, we thanked him and said that we would leave that night so as not to be a burden. He insisted that we stay, saying that we were no trouble and it was probably safer for us to stay with him.

After all, we were runaways and the police would be looking for us. He said that he was a cop, so no one would think to look for us there. We ended up staying, and I wish the story had turned out this way:

We are having a wonderful stay, and Bobby and his friends are really kind and helpful. Bobby falls in love with me, and we live together in his house like any boyfriend and girlfriend would. He is always eager and happy to see me, and keeps reminding me of how he took me in and looked after me. He tells me that if I really love him as much as he loves me I would not be afraid to share myself with him, and so I consent to become his lover.

I am only sixteen and a half years old and prefer to pretend that I am in love with my handsome prince. I have no concept of what love is, since I have been shoved around so much in my life, and I think sex is the way people show their respect and affection for each other.

The real story goes like this: We were forced to pay our way as prostitutes. Bobby brought his friends home with him night after night. The same men every night would spend hours drinking in the lounge and then have their way with my two friends. I was able to hold off from the other guys, as Bobby used me as his personal prostitute as long as I did not make a fuss. I hated who I became. I saw this disgusting creature that was selling her body and her loyalty to survive.

As my self-loathing grew, I wished I had the courage to walk out of the house and into oncoming traffic. But I didn't have the courage to do even that simple thing.

I got so thin I looked anorexic. The weight just dropped off me as each day passed. I hated eating their food and sleeping in their beds. I hated my friends, who couldn't or wouldn't say no, and most of all I hated me. I could not even find an excuse for us being there now, and so as I lay in the bed next to a man almost old enough to be my father I gave in and gave up.

It had been the longest week of my life, and I hated myself so much, I kept telling myself that this was all I deserved. And then one day I found myself confronted by two of the other guys that frequented Bobby's house. They would come and go as they pleased.

One tried to force himself onto me; threatening to throw me out and call the cops if I didn't play nicely. He pulled at my clothes and planted disgusting slobbery kisses all over me. He smelt like a stale beer bottle. I was doing my best to remain calm so as not to anger him. I felt sick to my stomach and just want to die. I made an excuse about needing the toilet, and then called the girls to me. My friend and I decided we had to get away. Neither of us could take another day in the house and no matter how we tried we could not convince the other girl to come with us.

We could not change her mind, but made her promise to stay in the bathroom until we had made our getaway. I was so over this disgusting way of living. My friend and I climbed out of the bathroom window and took off like bats out of hell.

With every step I took my self-loathing got stronger, and I decided I was no better than a whore. So if someone came along at that moment and picked us up, whatever happened would be God's will, his punishment for us. Even though I had disavowed religion, my old belief systems were so ingrained; it was only natural that I fell back on them. It never occurred to me that two teenage girls on the road were just the perfect pickings for some unscrupulous men.

We were picked up again, and this time we were taken into the country. There we lived with some hippies who, although they believed in free love for all, saw us for what we were: children. They never made any demands on us. How strange that people who are so highly respected in society could abuse their positions so blatantly, whereas those who were referred to as the dregs of society took care of us like the children we were. For the sake of this story, I will call them Jenny and Tommy.

This lovely couple had a beautiful pig. For the life of me I can't remember its name, but this was when I first discovered that I adored pigs and how loving they could be. He was so smart, and I would talk to him for ages. He became my friend, even though we were there for only four days.

On that fourth day, we saw Jenny and Tommy speeding towards us along their unpaved driveway, dust billowing up behind them and all but obscuring their car. They almost fell out of the car, rapidly telling us that the police were not too far behind and they knew that we were there. We needed to get going as quick as possible if we were going to avoid capture and ending up locked up in a cell somewhere at their mercy.

My friend and I knew exactly what it meant to be at the mercy of the Arm of the Law, and we fled immediately. Jenny and Tommy shoved some money into our hands and asked us to call them as soon as all had settled down. Harboring runaways in the sixties was just as bad a crime as kidnapping, so we made ourselves scarce.

By the time we made it to the highway, it was freezing and dark as hell. We discussed what we should do. Both of us had such low self-esteem now and had lost all the confidence we used to have. Besides that we hated ourselves and the life we had got caught up in. We wanted out. We were sick to our stomachs, and I could not even look at myself in the mirror in a public toilet. It made me feel ill just looking into my eyes.

We sat down and wept for what seemed like ages. We huddled together to keep ourselves warm, clinging to each other as if our lives depended on it. We had changed, everything had changed, and we had had enough. We wanted our parents, whom we did not even know that well, but any comfort at that moment was preferable to none.

We made a decision then and there to return to the school and damn the consequences. Even that was better than this life. At least we would not have to sell our souls to survive. We would just have to try to remain as inconspicuous as we could until it was time to move on from that place.

We turned around and went back the way we had come. A nice couple picked us up, and we told them that we had run away from home and that we had changed our minds. We said that our parents wouldn't have missed us yet, so we needed to get back as soon as we could so as not to upset them.

We looked afraid, tired, and totally miserable, and they fell for it. Being on the run required lying, but every time I told a lie, revulsion and loathing coursed through me. The couple offered to drive us all the way back home, and we promised to tell our parents that they had helped us. It was a pleasant trip back, even though there was no laughter, as we knew what we were going back to.

CHAPTER 12

The Return

TWO DAYS LATER AT three in the morning, we walked through the gate and knocked on the door of the hostel. We had managed to buy some alcohol and had been drinking for the last several hours. By the time we got to the hostel, we were roaring drunk and ready to take on the world. The alcohol had given us the courage we needed to face what we knew was to come.

We staggered to the door, and I literally fell against the doorbell. In the early hours of the morning, it sounded like a siren to us, and we laughed so hard as it woke the whole hostel. We were almost dragged inside and the headmaster was called.

Dirty old bugger, I thought as he prepared to beat us. *You probably get off on belting us girls across the backside.* Man, I swear he lifted his arm twice as high and almost levitated off the ground in his attempt to hit us as hard as he could. I can't even remember how many cuts we got and it did not matter. I was too drunk to care and too pissed off with life to think about it.

We were placed in the lock-up cells for three weeks. Talk about prison. I could not fathom how they came up with such a severe punishment, considering we had come back on our own. Three weeks without company can be pretty daunting, especially because we had no reading or writing materials, and jeez I missed my smokes.

Some of the other girls were caught and returned to the school, and things did not go well for them. Others never came back, and I wished them only the best.

I remained in that school for one year and then once again was transferred to another school. I lost contact with my beautiful friend and have never heard from her again. I send out love and blessings to her, and hope that she too had the good fortune to discover what I did about life and all that it encompasses.

I remained at that school until I was seventeen. Each day I became stronger and more determined to survive that place, where they held children in contempt and used us as their personal whipping girls to overcome their own inadequacies.

I kept my focus on passing my exams so that one way or another, I would be released from this school or transferred to another one. Anything had to be better than the place I was living now.

It felt to me as if I was missing out on the best years of my life. I had not been to a dance for so many years. I had forgotten what it was like to go to the movies, to go to the local roadhouse and have a milkshake or listen to a jukebox. I had not taken a walk in town, ridden a bike, or tried to roller skate. I had never had the opportunity to be a child. Almost seventeen years old, I felt like I was fifty.

Discovery or Destruction

We are human, and as we grow up we are reminded that our pasts have a direct bearing on who we will become as adults. With this disempowering thought firmly planted in our subconscious minds, we cling to our childhood memories as if they are our lifeblood.

We sit in our rooms all alone and go over and over all the saddest and most debilitating moments of our youth. We weep and stew over them, building an ever-growing resentment towards those who, in our minds, are responsible for the bad things that happened to us.

Hate and fear become our constant companions. We blame others for each poor choice we make. We keep remembering the past, holding onto unhappy memories, thinking that with the sympathy of those around us, we can continue to place the blame on the world and the shoulders of society.

We don't have to take responsibility for any of it. All we have to do is let it go. Use any of it that strengthens us, benefits us, and teaches us. All that has gone before no longer has any bearing on who we are becoming.

When people hear about my life, they always want to know how I managed to live through it. They say things like, "I would have committed suicide or crawled into a dark place and never come out again." There were days when I did almost try to kill myself, and other days when I crawled into a very dark place in my mind. But those times never made me feel good or worthy of who I was.

Despite what had happened, and because of it, I decided that no matter what, I would grow up to be a good and empowered person. I made it my business to take charge of each and every decision I made about my life.

My ego is my greatest challenge these days, but mostly I have a firm handle on it. Some say that I talk about myself in the third person and surely that must mean I am nuts. I say to them that if that is the case, then I am the happiest nut they will ever meet.

CHAPTER 13

As the Wheels Turn

AFTER HAVING SPENT THE holidays with my mother stepfather and sister who I had not seen since I was eleven years old I returned to the reformatory school before being sent to yet another school. This new school was exactly the same as the one I had just been transferred from.

While on holiday I had met a man twenty years older than me through friends of my parents. I had mistakenly thought that I could date the guy and that he would treat me respectfully because my parents knew him. What a joke he got me drunk gave me drugs and raped me

I kept blaming the things I did on my upbringing. Why should I take responsibility for what happened to me? Why not lay the blame at the door of society? Then I could continue to make a hash of things without taking charge of my life.

The new school was pretty much the same as the last one. The hostels and the school were on the same premises. Each girl was assigned to a hostel, and only the staff knew what the requirements were for placement. I had been shown my dormitory, and there was hardly any difference between this one and the last one, this hostel had two floors and I was in the upstairs section. An open-plan corridor separated the dining room, kitchen, and staff quarters from one another.

There were about twenty girls in each room, and the beds were a little higher than in the last place. Sort of like hospital beds without the ability to wind up or down. Sheets and one blanket were folded at the foot of the bed, inviting me to make it. Every girl had a locker and a metal wardrobe, just the same as the other school. Here too we were given government-issue clothes to wear. No personal clothes allowed.

Two beds away from where I was to sleep was a bed that was unmade with a badly stained mattress on it. As it was closer to the window I asked if I could swop the mattress with the one that had been allocated to me. The girl that had ushered me to my bed laughed nervously and said: "do whatever you like, but I must warn you the girl that used to sleep in that bed cut her own throat and bled to death in that bed over night. No one has ever been able to approach that bed since." Point taken I made my bed up right where it was and got out of that room as quick as I could.

No one was quite sure of the reason the matron of the hostel chose to leave the mattress on that bed. Morbid curiosity always seems to get the better of us humans.

As with the other school, each girl was allocated certain chores. One difference was that although we had to wash the floors and put the polish on by hand, at least this school had floor polishers to shine the floors with. That gave our backs and knees a little respite. To this day I am unable to kneel for longer than a minute, and even then it hurts like the blazes. I have blamed my bad knees on my life experiences, because then I could point a finger at someone else and say, "Your fault."

One of the worst jobs was peeling potatoes. We did not have peelers, so we had to do it with a knife, and the skin peels had to be so thin, you could almost see through them. If they were thick the houseparent would make you boil them up and that would be your lunch. I got good at peeling potatoes, I can tell you. All the dishes were washed by hand, so even before you got to school, you were worn out already.

In the morning, after assembly but before school started, we would all have to line up with our hands stretched out before us. The headmaster would then do the rounds, inspecting our fingers to see if we had smoked either cigarettes or marijuana.

If your hands were discolored, you were punished and privileges were taken from you. For example, you wouldn't be able to attend church or, if you were in one of the top groups, go to town. Although none of us were religious, we loved going to church as this gave us the freedom we needed to buy smokes or get some weed off the local boys that attended church.

There was plenty of misuse of medication too, and even though the rules were very strict about not bringing drugs in, you could always find something when feeling at your lowest ebb.

We were incredibly inventive when it came to hiding the smokes, since we were searched when we came back from anywhere that was outside the gates. Going to town was for the girls that had acquired the *A* status through creeping and living within the conformity and limitations placed upon them.

They never questioned anything and always dobbed you in if you did anything that looked like "higher status" points to them.

I don't think I ever got out of the *EE* group because I wanted to question everything and was as cheeky as all buggery. I was never a "yes sir, no sir" person, and even to this day I live my life according to what makes me feel good and not what makes someone else happy. I spent almost every weekend scrubbing the writing off the wooden desks of the entire school.

Corporal punishment was meted out across the hands with a cane, and I am sure the headmaster tried his very best to get the bone at the base of the thumb with each lash.

I had been there a couple of months when I experienced my first earth tremor. We were in the classroom during exams, when suddenly there was a rattling noise, as if everything was shaking. And then everything was. We were first told to get under the desks and then we were led from the classroom to the yard. It also happened one night very late, and there was no time to grab dressing gowns. Each time we had to wait outside until they were sure the tremors were over. It was pretty scary, but not as fearful as it would have been if they'd been strong enough to cause destruction, as earthquakes did in other parts of the world.

I don't know if the reason I disliked school so much was because of the circumstances of my life. My IQ was a little above average, yet I could not be bothered with school. We were forced to do secretarial subjects, like mercantile law, typing, shorthand, and bookkeeping.

How boring this all was to me. I loved languages, writing, and singing, those kinds of things. I was a dreamer, and I always used my dreams to escape from the horror and menace of these schools.

We were ruled with the strictest of rules, and if you broke them in any way, they would either lock you up in a little room or not allow any contact with your family and friends. I had no family within the vicinity, so mostly I was locked up.

One of my favorite songs to sing was called "Try and catch the Wind," by Donovan. The lyrics were written on the wall of my regular cell. I would sing this song over and over when I was on the outside, and so would the other girls who were put in that cell. The walls were covered with all sorts of graffiti, just like you'd see in jail cells in movies.

I was once placed in the cells because I was supposed to spy on some of the girls who were suspected of being lesbians. I was told I had to inform the headmaster of their activities and whether the girls sleeping together in the same bed.

Two or three of those girls were good friends of mine, and their sexual preferences made no difference to me. It was, as far as I was concerned, none of my business. Still, I was told I would have to remain in the cell until I wrote a report about the other girls, and that this was being done in the other hostels. I refused to spy on my fellow students and so I remained confined in the cell. Goodness only knows how long I may have stayed there but as usual life and its circumstances intervened.

CHAPTER 14

Live and Let Live

I HAD BEEN IN the cell for approximately one week when I opened my eyes in the middle of the night and saw my stepfather standing at the door to my cell. I thought I was dreaming. He had a lovely smile on his face, and although I could not hear a voice, I got the feeling he was saying good-bye.

I blinked, and he seemed to fade into the wall. I thought that at last, after being locked up in all these places since I was four, I was losing my mind. These horrible people were going to have the last laugh. They would lock me in an asylum, where they had sent so many other kids. I vowed never to tell anyone what I had seen, not even the girls that I liked. In this place, you never knew when your best friend would turn on you just to get extra privileges.

Late the next night the matron of the hostel opened my cell door. I could not believe it. How had she found out? I had not even been in contact with anyone.

She informed me that the headmaster wanted to see me in his office. I was panicking. I did not know what to think. They never came to get you out this late at night. What the hell was I going to do now? Maybe I could just break away from the matron and run as fast and far as my legs would carry me.

I entered the office and was confused even more when the headmaster stood up and told me to take a seat. He asked if I wanted some water and then sat down himself. Well, by now I was terrified. Why was he talking so nicely to me?

He wanted to know what contact I'd had with my mother before I arrived there. He asked if my mother had been ill. The last time I had seen my mother I had been eighteen and all had been well with her. My stepfather was seven years younger than my mother so I was more concerned about my mother than him.

"Is there something wrong with my mother?" I asked frantically.

He assured me we would get to that question in due course.

What the hell did that mean? Was she sick or not? What the heck was going on? He asked about my stepfather. By now I was shaking so much inside, I felt incoherent. What was he trying to say? Were my parent's dead? Was that what this was all about? But I was just too scared to ask and sat there like a stunned mullet.

He wanted to know if my stepfather had been ill. How would I know? I was not thinking coherently at the time I had been locked up for a week in isolation. I never got any correspondence from my mother. I could not even tell him the color of her hair or how old she was. Well I did know that she was sixteen years older than me and the last time I saw her she had brown hair. My mother constantly colored her hair. I think at the time I was terrified of what I was about to hear and my thoughts were so scattered. Why could he not get on with it? What was he trying find out? Had they done something wrong?

Suddenly he looked at me and said in a blunt voice that sounded like it was being forced through a hollow pipe, "Your stepfather is dead. He died this morning at seven a.m."

I looked at him as if he were nuts, because my stepfather was only twenty-eight years old. Surely he must have had the wrong information. It suddenly dawned on me that this man seemed to be enjoying himself at my expense. I was behaving so out of character for me. I was always so in control of my emotions, yet here I as now thinking and saying things that made no sense at all.

I said something like, "Are you sure? He's still so young." There were no tears. I just looked at him, and then said, "Oh" when he nodded his head.

I was taken back to the hostel instead of the cell and told to go to bed. When I got upstairs to my dorm, some of the girls were awake. Since this was a most unusual situation, they asked what was up.

"My father just died, I think," was all I could manage to say before getting into bed and falling asleep almost immediately. This never happened to me. I had not fallen asleep before at least three a.m. ever since I was nine years old.

I am still not sure that I ever cried, but now I had to come clean and informed my friends that I was pregnant. I mentioned earlier in the chapter that during a brief stay with my mother some months earlier, I had got to know an older man, a friend of a friend of my stepfathers. Having no real experience with men, I had fallen prey to this unscrupulous man and now found myself to be pregnant. I was taken to a doctor to verify the fact, and then plans were set in motion to send me to a home for unwed mothers to have my baby.

Matron and the Headmaster where aware that I had fallen pregnant. My parents had been informed by mail that this was the case. None of the girls or other staff were privy to this information. I am not sure if it was due to the fact that girls that were pregnant were not allowed to be in lockup.

During an argument with my mother months later she told me that my stepfather had been diagnosed with cancer of the bowl when he was only 19 years old. He had crashed a truck that had been previously used to carry asbestos and become ill a few months later.

There were many secrets that unfolded over the next few years and as I mentioned earlier in the book about my stepfather's erratic behavior this was the excuse my mother gave for his having threatened her with the gun.

I was not sent back to the lockups again. The best thing was that I had not betrayed the confidence of my friends.

CHAPTER 15

A New Chapter

I FAILED MY EXAMS abysmally, but then I didn't even try. I just wanted out of these disgusting places that tried to take not only your dignity but also your very soul. I hated the staff, the girls for just giving in, and especially the welfare agency with such intensity, the feeling sometimes would make my head reel.

The day I got on the train and left that place I vowed that whatever it took, I would never allow this to happen to my own children. I never looked back, and for the most part I never even gave my past a thought. It was my intention to sweep it all under the carpet, as if it had never happened.

I arrived back in my hometown. My mother was there with another woman and a beautiful blond guy with a little girl between him and the welfare woman. My mother and the other woman were talking as they approached me. I could feel the other woman's energy and knew she was from welfare. I despised her before she was even introduced to me. I had left all my feelings behind in the orphanage when I was locked in the first cupboard. From now on I was in control of my life, and I felt sorry for anyone who tried to get in my way.

The handsome young man turned out to be my brother, whom I had not seen in years. The little girl was my sister.

Two other children were missing from the fold and I did not even care. All I knew was that I was out of those places and that I was about to become a mother. I was afraid that since I had lost all feeling, I would not love the child. The welfare agency had decided I could stay with my mother instead of going to a home, so I moved in with her and my siblings until it was time for me to have the child.

CHAPTER 16
Freedom

I AM FREE. THE chains of bondage have been broken. No longer can other people tell me what I can and can't do, where to go, what to eat, who to see and what I can believe. That was what I thought the moment I stepped off the train and into a free society.

I quickly realized how wrong I was. Life did not turn out as I had expected. I was free, so why did it feel worse than ever before?

One day while my mother and I were visiting some of her friends and they all had a few drinks. I made some comment about the drinking, and my mother called me a slut and told me to keep my mouth shut. She insinuated that if she did not know the truth about my baby's father, she would have suspected the baby was my stepfather's.

I looked at her in disgust and mumbled, "Like mother, like daughter."

She walked right up to me and slapped my face hard.

I spat out words to the effect of, "Don't you ever hit me again. I am my own boss now."

"If you ever talk to me like that again," she said, "I will slap you in the mouth again, even if you are sixty."

I believe she would too. At that moment I did not like my mother very much even though I loved her more than words can say.

She had even accused me of causing my stepfather's death, saying that when he read the letter from school that I was pregnant, he lost his footing and fell down the steps, thereby aggravating his already deadly disease.

I did not feel anything but contempt for her attempting to put the blame on me. I was used to this kind of treatment, so it meant squat to me. It just confirmed that this world was a dog eat dog world, and that I would have to be as hard as nails to survive.

I had been home for two and a half months and was preparing for the birth of my new baby. It was almost as if I had been given the chance to relive my life through the eyes of a child. I was so afraid I would be unable to love him enough. What if I turned out to be an awful mother? What if there was something wrong with him? What if I died while giving birth? After all, the matron at school had told me that as punishment for Eve stealing the apple and misleading Adam with her evil ways, God had made giving birth so painful that many women died from the agony.

I had only just got out into the free world, so I didn't want to die yet. *I won't die,* I vowed to myself. I would be so strong I wouldn't feel a thing. My child would not bring me any pain; no one would ever make me feel pain again. Not the pain of the flesh or the pain of the soul. I would lock my heart away in a place so obscure and dark, no one would ever find it. Only I would know where it was and I would never ever tell anyone. It would be a secret until the day I died.

My mother had met up with an old sweetheart, George. She told me they had been in love before my father came along. She said my dad had been so handsome and charming, he had stolen her heart away from this man. Well, what do you expect? Most people's heart are so fickle anyway, so she was not that much different from everyone else. George asked us to come and live with him in his house. At that time we were living in the back rooms of someone else's house. At least it was better than being in an orphanage.

CHAPTER 17

A Funny Man

WE MOVED INTO GEORGE'S semidetached house. His neighbors were two single brothers, and they had two Alsatian dogs. George's African maid was drunk all the time and called my mother Mummy. What a strange household. George had three kids living with him as well, a daughter who was extremely overweight and two sons. The younger son was fifteen and seemed terribly insecure, while the older one seemed to have a chip on his shoulder all the time. George also had two beautiful dogs, and one joined in when you sang to him.

The house was fairly old but comfortable. The kitchen had a sloping floor, almost as if it had been made that way to make sure that any water in the kitchen would run out. All the mice would come up through a hole in the floor and then depart again, laden with anything that was left out for consumption. As soon as he saw the mice, George's dog Tick would take off like a frog in a sock and would hide behind the door with just his nose sticking out. As soon as he saw the mice he chased them, his nose to the floor, he would lose traction on the vinyl floor and slide across the room until his nose ended up in the mouse hole under the basin. It was so funny to watch. I loved that dog. He was such a character.

There was a strange air about George's house, and I always got the feeling I was being watched. A passage ran from the front door and straight to the back door, with one small step halfway between the two doors.

George had a cigarette and matches collection (mostly matches) that came from every country in the world. He had placed them all neatly on a straw mat hanging on a wall in the lounge. The fireplace in that room was the original one, there since the house was built. It was a beautiful sight to behold. I have always had an appreciation of antiques and have decided that one day I will furnish my dream home with them.

My mum and George's room had a bay window with a verandah that ran across the length of the front of the house. George told us that he wanted to put a swimming pool outside the window where their bed was, so that he could just roll over and right into the pool. Then he would not have to have a bath. He was by far one of the funniest people I knew.

One day he put on an old karate suit, complete with its black belt, and said that he was an expert. He went out onto the front lawn and took up the stance. We all stood rooted to the spot, in awe of what we were about to witness. He lifted his leg in the air, shot it forward, and then brought it down. He let out a yell of pain. He had stepped right into a bush of thorns and now had them stuck in his foot. There he was, leg in the air, doing the bunny hop on one leg. Oh God, it was so funny to see the look on his face when he saw us laughing. All he could say was, "I'll get you for this."

On another day we were all sitting in the lounge. George was in his favorite chair, and beside him was the table on which he would put his favorite glass. The glass was green with a pattern on it and a handle. Mum had just given him a drink, and they were teasing each other about something. He put his glass down on the table and said, "Jumping Jesus." As he said this, the glass jumped up, spilled its contents and then settled back on the table. It was so funny, but I can safely tell you that he never ever said those words again until the day he died. Especially in the house where Jumping Jesus obviously resided.

It was so easy to laugh in that house, but for all that I was always weary and on my guard. I had trusted people before and no good had come from it.

I was well into my pregnancy now and Christmas had come and gone. It was the best one I had ever had because I was not only with my mother, sister, and brother, but I had received a present for the first time in eight years, since I was eleven years old. It was a dress that looked like Joseph's Technicolored dream coat. There was no way in the world I would ever wear it, but I treasured it until my sister Tanis was discovered.

CHAPTER 18

An Angel Comes to Visit

I HAD BEEN FEELING strange for a few days and I believed I needed to go to the hospital. It seemed as if I had gone into labor, but the contractions were far apart. I told my mother, and to be on the safe side, we thought it would be best to go see a doctor.

Good thing I went. The doctor suspected I may have developed some kind of infection, and he decided I had to be induced for the safety of the child. He informed me that they were trying a new medication that would induce the labor as well as halve the time of the contractions. He said it might work immediately, or take a little longer, or not work at all. He assured me that either way; there would be no ill effects where the baby was concerned.

The nurse, under the supervision of the doctor, injected the serum. It was a slow process. As I watched I could see my blood mingle with the serum and then slowly drain back into me. It took a few minutes, and when it was over the doctor told the nurse to give me lunch while we waited to see what would happen.

I turned a nice shade of pale as I felt the contractions start and blurted out that I didn't think I'd have time for lunch. The doctor asked in surprise, "Whatever do you mean?" and then understood as he looked at my face. It was 12.30 p.m. on 24 March, and I had gone into labor. He told the nurse to keep an eye on me and time my contractions. I kept feeling as if I needed the toilet and there was a constant sensation of needing to push. Please keep in mind that this was my first child and according to what I'd been told all my life, God did not like me because I had sinned.

I remember that Ringo Star was singing "It Don't Come Easy" as I walked through the theatre doors to the delivery room, and I forced a smile in acknowledgement. I heard a woman screaming loudly and muttering in what I thought was Italian. The nurse said something about Italian woman believing that the louder you screamed, the bigger and healthier the baby would be. I just thought that screaming hurt my throat.

My baby was born at 5.00 p.m. that day. The nurse bundled him up and would not let me see him.

"It's a boy," she said. "For now you need your rest, and someone will be in to see you shortly. You will be given a needle that will make you a little drowsy, but all will be well when you wake up. You have to have many stitches, which is most unusual."

I don't know how long I waited for them to come in with my baby, but when the doctor and a woman came in, there was no baby with them. The woman had some papers in her hand. She smiled brightly at me and said, "I just want you to sign these papers, Linda, so that we can give the baby to his new mommy."

I looked at this woman through drowsy and foggy eyes and said, "But I'm his new mommy."

"Not anymore," she said. "We have a new mommy waiting outside to take him home."

These words came to me as if through a tunnel that had wadding in it. I tried to shake my head, but it would not do what I wanted it to.

The woman placed the papers on the little breakfast trolley in front of me. She put a pen in my hand, set my hand on the papers, and whispered impatiently, "Sign them now or you will never see your son."

I started to wail, very loudly, and one by one I saw heads turn towards me. It felt as if no sound was coming out of my mouth as I cried, "I want my baby. Where's my mother? I want my baby."

The woman and the doctor seemed to disappear into thin air. Someone was telling me to calm down as everything was all right now. They were going to bring me my baby.

I am not sure but I think I fell asleep, and when I woke up to the nurse was holding my baby. He was wrapped in blankets but had not even been washed yet. He was still covered with the fluids of afterbirth. She placed him in my arms, and he sort of dropped to the bed.

When I removed the blankets, there was this tiny, tiny boy with golden hair that seemed very long for a newborn. He was a mere four pounds, four ounces. He was so perfect in every way, looking up at me with his little eyes.

My heart seemed to swell in my chest. I felt light-headed as tears of joy spilled over my cheeks and landed on his little face. I placed my face close to him and felt the warmth of his tiny body emanate upward to me, drawing from me a love so pure, so all encompassing, that I gasped in delight, as if I had just tasted something so sweet, so divinely mouthwatering.

Here was a tiny angel that needed me, who would love me without question and trust me with his life. I had a responsibility to be the best mommy I knew how to be. I would love and cherish him and protect him with my life. I would try to give him all those things I had missed out on. I would never let anyone take him away from me.

I was a mother now, filled with fear, confusion, and excitement. I had never been told how to be a mother. I knew nothing about changing nappies, feeding babies, or what would be required of me. I went on instinct alone, just as mothers would have thousands of years ago. They had all done a good job, so I could too.

I stayed in the hospital for seven days, which was normal in those days. My mother and George visited me as often as they could, and I could see that they were over the moon in love with my beautiful angel.

On one such visit, I was in the lounge with the baby when they arrived. George walked into the empty nurses station and slipped on a white coat and draped a stethoscope around his neck. It was so funny as he started prancing around, calling himself doctor. He followed me through to the maternity ward, still in his doctor's attire, and as he entered the ward he said, "Good morning, ladies. Time for your checkups." Everyone was cracking up, and those who did not know that he was just a visitor made us laugh even more by their reactions to what was happening.

He was such an entertainer and loved to make people laugh. My bed was set right next to the windows, which overlooked the ocean. Because of the height, it looked as if the window opened out to the sea itself. One day George started opening the window, mumbling, "I think I might just go for a quick swim." Some of the newer ladies were horrified, as we were about sixteen floors up.

I returned home to George and Mum's house and was informed by the welfare agency that I had to start working as soon as possible if I was going to provide a proper home for my son. I was not even sure yet what his name was going to be. My mother had told me that my stepfather's dying wish was for me to name the child Sean Michael, but I was not sure if my mum was being truthful.

She had said some pretty mean things to me in my life, and we were sorting them out at that time. Of course, we did not really know each other that well enough. My mother is wonderful, but she is just a human with her own issues that she was dealing with at the time. She had had one lousy life, I can tell you.

CHAPTER 19
Naming Game

My FIRST NIGHT BACK, I was still sharing a room with George's daughter Lola. There was a door between her room and the room George and my mother shared. For the moment, my baby was to sleep in there, as there was no room for his cot in the tiny room we shared.

I was finding it hard to go to sleep because I wanted to be with my baby, so as soon as everyone was asleep, I crept into my mum's room to get my baby. If anyone woke up, I would say he needed a feeding or a nappy change. I lay with him in my arms for hours, just breathing in his beautiful fragrance and keeping my lips touching his cheek all the time. His breathing was almost as fast as his heartbeat, but the nurse had told me that babies' hearts beats much faster than ours.

It must have been about three in the morning when I placed him back in his cot. He did not even murmur he was so sound asleep. I always had to wake him to give him a feed after about six hours at night, since he would not wake up on his own. Before I left him, I promised him that I would have his name by the time everyone woke up in the morning, so that we could stop calling him all sorts of strange names.

Back in my bed, I lay there wondering if I would ever break the habit of staying awake half the night, when I felt as if someone was pushing my arms, which were tucked under my head. I tried to open my eyes to see what was going on, but found that my eyelids seemed glued shut. I started to feel panic and tried to call out, but no sound came from my mouth. By now the weight was on my chest as well and I could not even move. What was going on? There was no getting away from it. The more I struggled, the worse it got, until I was sure I would suffocate. I thought about my baby in the next room and told myself that I would name him Michael. It stopped. The pressure lifted, and as I gazed into the dark, there was no one there. As quickly as it had started, it had stopped. If I had any doubts about my stepfather's last wish, that experience dispelled them completely. I know he had come to confirm what my mother had told me. In the morning I told my mother what had happened. I am not sure if she believed me, but it was clear as daylight to me that I had experienced something very extraordinary.

Michael was about four months old when I had to share a room with my brother. He was young and did not spend much time in the room. I did not mind, as I was used to sharing my rooms with at least nineteen other girls. One night I could not fall asleep, as usual. The electric fuse in the house had blown, so I had a candle next to my bed, on a small stool with my radio and a book. The pram that Michael was sleeping in was next to my bed so that I could be near him.

I was dreaming. My face was so hot, and someone was saying, "Linda, wake up, there is a fire." I rolled over in my bed, and the heat became intense. I could still hear the voice in my head: "Wake up, Linda, wake up. There's a fire." I turned over slowly and almost put my face right into the flames. I automatically pushed Michael's pram forward, since it had moved right up over the flames, and woke my brother. Between the two of us we put the fire out. All the time I was aware that Michael was okay and that there was nothing burning on or around the pram. I was amazed that there was no damage, since the fire it had been burning directly under the pram, right where Michael's head was. Because of the burning candle, the radio had melted, and the stool and book were so badly burnt, they had to be thrown away. There was no evidence the pram had been that close to a fire, even though it was made of some kind of vinyl.

I picked Michael up and went to my mother's room to wake her. Luckily George was working night shift. I told her what had happened as I sat down next to her. In the light, I lifted the blanket away from Michael's face. There he was, his face was pitch-black from smoke. All you could see were these little white eyes and the pink tongue in his mouth. He had the cutest smile, and we just broke down laughing with relief. He was fine and that was all that mattered. We never did tell George what had happened.

George adored Michael, probably because his relationship with his own children was always so shaky. Michael loved him too, and some nights he would refuse to sleep until his papa got home. Together they would sit up late at night and eat curry and ice cream together. Michael would fall asleep as soon as the treat was over and not wake up until morning. Michael was such a contented baby, and from day one he slept through the night. My friends would ask me why I always looked so fresh and full of life, even though I had a baby. I must say spending time with Michael and playing with him so much during the time I had with him tired him out pretty much.

If I had been able to have my way, I would have spent every moment of every day with him. It was such a delight to be needed and loved by someone without conditions placed on me. I was his mother and that was all he knew. Love and caring was all he needed, besides being fed and clothed.

Children are so uncomplicated and innocent. There are no expectations of us, and that is why it is so easy to give everything of one's self to a child. It is only when a child grows up and starts to receive biased and critical feedback from adults that they become limited in their thinking and actions. We criticize people that we do not even know, when we have no concept of what their lives have been like, and we expect them to conform to our way of thinking or doing things. It makes no sense to allow someone else the power to make you feel anything. They didn't come here to make us happy. They, like we, came here to complete a journey that they set forth for themselves on this earth.

Our children are so precious and have chosen to come here to help us with our journeys. The very least we can do is not fill their heads with our personal fears and disillusionment, and allow them to make choices for themselves based on unconditional love. After all, love is why we came here and love is what binds us all together. We are unique beings, but never separate.

CHAPTER 20

Who Do You Trust?

I GOT A JOB and we had found a wonderful woman of African descent to take care of Michael while I was at work. I worked for the government, so the pay was on time and regular. I had to give almost every penny to my mother and George for board and lodging, but we had a roof over our heads, beds to sleep in, and food to eat. Money meant nothing to me at that time, as I was so focused on giving my baby a good home.

I had decided that I would forgo any type of social life, since my aim was very clear to me. Michael was all that mattered, especially because someone had told me that his father had died and no one seemed to know anything about him. What he had told me about himself could have been true or not. He knew about the baby, yet he never contacted me. I was on my own in this, and that was how I wanted it to stay.

I threw myself into my work and being a good mother to Michael. One day I returned home early from work. As I entered the house, I heard my mother talking to someone. She was saying, "Come on, Come to Mommy." Perplexed, I followed the voice and saw my Mother holding her hand out to Michael who was in his pram. The words she was saying were directed to him.

I felt myself becoming hot as if my blood were boiling. I had trusted her with my child, and now this was happening. I spoke to Doris, the woman I had hired to look after Michael, and she told me my mother had been doing this for some two months now, and was also encouraging Michael to call George Daddy. I was furious, and then she gave me the news that would change everything between my mother and me for a long time to come. She told me that my mother and George had been talking with the welfare agency, and that they had signed some papers requesting to adopt my little boy. I just looked at her in horror and then took my baby and went for a walk. I knew I had to get away from my mother for a while.

I walked around, trying to gain my composure even as it felt like the world was about to come crashing down around me. I started to shake and realized that if I did not pull myself together, I would lose any composure I had left and start screaming. I looked at my beautiful little angel and made up my mind to find someone to take us out of that house and into a home of our own.

I returned home. My mother was waiting, and so was George. My mum started making excuses at first, and then she tried to deny everything, but I could see that now that they had been found out, they were coming undone. Mum started shouting at me and crying. I told her I would never be able to trust her again. She began calling me names, like whore, and told me I had no morals. The look I gave her was her undoing. She grabbed me from behind and pinned my arms behind me as her weight forced me to sit on my bed.

I could not believe what was happening. I was back in the Girls Reformatory School, and the next thing I knew George laid into me, punching me, never touching my face, just hitting me in the chest and stomach. I know Doris witnessed this, but because of her position in the house, she had no recourse but to walk away. Her job depended on her silence, and she knew that. The pain was excruciating, and my breasts felt as if they were going numb. I had never hated two people more in my life than I did those two at that moment. All I could hear were her words: "Hit her, George. Hit her where it hurts. Hit her, hit her, hit her." She just kept repeating the words over and over, and he did not stop until she did.

Eight months had passed since that awful day. Once again everyone had clamed up and the incident was never mentioned again. There was a great deal of strain between my mother and myself and the laughter and fun had evaporated into an uncomfortable and stifled atmosphere between the three of us.

Everything had changed now and I started showing interest in dating. I was only interested in a social life for purely selfish reasons. I never asked my mother to take care of my baby again instead I got our trusted home help to babysit him in her home. After a few months I met one of my brother's friends James who spent a lot of time at our house and I made myself irresistible to him. All I wanted was for someone to take me away from the place I was in and take care of my baby and me.

We dated for a month and then he asked me to come and live with him. I grabbed at that straw with both hands so that I could get out of the house. I did not hate my mother any longer. I just felt pity for her. She had destroyed an already shaky relationship between us, and now I was not even sure I wanted to have a relationship with her at all. I am not sure what transpired between my mother and the adoption agency but nothing further ever came of it.

I moved out of the house and into my boyfriend's apartment. I got another job working in a supermarket. It was close to home, so that my home help could bring Michael in to visit me during the day, and then bring him after work so that I could walk home with him at the end of the day.

My boyfriend was a bookkeeper and earned a good wage. I also liked his brothers and mother very much. They were always so nice to me. I was not in love with him, and physically all men left me cold because of the experiences I had had. But I played the role well, and this kept a roof over our heads and food in Michael's belly every day. He was also very kind to my baby, and that was a big plus.

I didn't see much of my mother at that time, but we did have coffee together. We never spoke about what had happened. I forgave my mother in time, since she was just working through her own problems and I had been separated from her long enough. I learnt to appreciate the fact that deep down inside she was a beautiful soul with a lot on her plate. I also believed that her drinking had a lot to do with her inability to cope with some situations. I know that George had given her an ultimatum to give up drinking or give up him.

Am I making excuses for her? Maybe. But I know she loved me irrespective of what had happened. I never told my brother or little sister about what happened that day. It really had nothing to do with them. It was something my mother and I would have to work through in our own time. George continued on as if nothing had happened, but I could now understand his relationship with his own children. It was not very good, and there was a great deal of upheaval and anger between them all.

So this was my induction into society. After having spent fourteen years in one orphanage after another, I felt as if I had walked straight into hell. I was in turmoil, afraid, insecure, unhappy, and all alone. There seemed to be not one person that I could trust, not even my mother.

When my day was over and I was by myself, I would devour book after book. Searching for answers, hoping to find some information that would give me some purpose in life. I had a baby now, and I wanted him to have a better start in life.

I needed to find my personal truth so that I could teach my boy from a different perspective. There had to be something more. It took many years of reading and listening, failing and succeeding, before it all fell into place for me.

CHAPTER 21

Freedom Is a Perspective

WHY IS IT THAT in the most difficult of circumstances, some people can feel happy, while others who are in what appears to be perfect circumstances are utterly miserable?

This is where the questions come into play, and we become so confused about our responsibilities and where they lie. If you look closely at the issue you would get a scenario like this:

All those people in my life need to change the things they are doing, believe what I believe, see what I see, feel what I feel, and behave in a way that will make me happy.

On the other hand, it is my responsibility to change what I am doing, believe what everyone around me believes, see what they see, feel what they feel, and behave according to what makes them happy.

Can you see how this does not make any sense? Why would we come into this time-space reality as ourselves? Why don't we come as someone else? Would it make any difference to what we believe? I think not, as we will still be confronted by the same issues that society says we need to adhere to.

This reads like a real comedy, and that our lives have become "a real comedy of disempowerment and limitations." We continue to allow those around us to tell us how to live our lives.

We may as well give them a pen and paper and ask them to write the story of our lives, so that we can make sure we don't step outside of the box of what makes them happy. We can sit back and live the life of anger, frustration, unhappiness, and poverty according to our friends, family, and neighbor's.

If your neighbor's plants die, they can blame you and say that had you reminded them to water the plants, they would have survived.

You can give up a cruise or holiday because someone in the family is unwell and everyone is afraid he or she will die while you are away.

You can forgo the opportunity to invest in something that will bring you financial security because your clairvoyant says you should not trust your feelings.

Are you able to see where I am going with this line of thought? You can never be miserable enough, unhappy enough, poor enough, or sick enough to make someone else joyous, happy, rich, or well. You would need to place your life on hold while everyone around you expects that all the other people they know will do the same.

How can you then ever expect to have one single moment of fulfillment? You would be run ragged in your endeavor to bring happiness and joy to the whole world, while you live in misery and poverty.

These are the things I have learnt from all the experiences I had as a child growing up in a society of conformity and limitations. Religion, dogma, and politics play such an overwhelming part in our lives because of the things we are taught from the perspective of someone else's life.

As my life unfolded before me from the perspective of my houseparent's, the staff, the teacher who became pregnant, the directors of the homes who were so different from one another, the confusion removed me farther from my connection to God Source. I therefore allowed them to taint my perspective of life through my not knowing who I really was.

Each time they experienced unhappiness, they would teach me from that perspective. Each time they made a choice that delivered a consequence they did not like, they taught me how to react when confronted by that same situation. Never once did they consider that what may appear wrong or right to them might not apply to me.

Each and every one of us has a different journey, and even though some of our experiences are shared by the people we connect with, ultimately they become part of our story because of the choices we made. We draw into our lives all the people, circumstances, and situations we encounter by how we choose to respond to what is going on around us.

Had I known this as a child, I would have been empowered to make choices from my personal perspective. I am not saying that everything about my life would have changed, just that I would have been able to cope from a more empowering point of view. I would have been able to make choices that might have made it easier for me to decide what was good or bad for me personally. However, I would not have had the opportunity to share with you, the reader, a view from a different perspective.

CHAPTER 22

Sifting through the Contrast

Memories that are pressed between the pages of my mind, searching for memories to bring a smile. Now is my time. Linda Lang

THIS WAS A TIME for me to start over, to release the old and discover new ways of creating beautiful memories. I stand before the mirror, and as memories flit across my face, showing all the different masks of days gone by, I shudder and try to lock them out.

I stare bewildered at this person looking back at me. My eyes scour the face, trying to get inside the mind. I see fear, angst, sadness, and aloneness. At first I allow these feeling to come and go as they please. I encourage the memories to spill over like a dam when the sluice gates have been opened.

The feelings begin to change from cold and unyielding. A warm feeling starts to course through my body, and I tremble. Who is this looking back at me, what does she want from me, and why do her eyes cry out for release? What can I do?

I can see the memories flowing from the mirror like a mudslide. At first the mud is dark and thick like clay, as large boulders crumble around my feet. I am rooted to the spot, and now I feel like I am standing in quicksand. The mud is up to my thighs and I can't move. I try to place a hold on the memories spilling forth, but it is too late. I have to go with them or drown.

My mind cries out, "I don't want to drown. I don't want to die. I don't want to go to the hell of the damned." I want to be free to make new memories. I want to fly like a bird that soars high above the so-called troubles of the world and see the beauty and awesomeness of a world where love is predominant and fear does not exist.

The color of the mud is changing, and there are fewer and fewer boulders. I look into my eyes, and they stare back at me as if they were floating under water. A river is now running down my face, and as I place my hand on my cheek, I realize I am crying for the first time in years.

The mud is becoming like chocolate, smooth and milky. Or like coffee, creamy and frothy. The tears keep coming. My whole body aches as it shakes uncontrollably, as if it is shaking off the hurts and pain of time gone by.

Suddenly the coffee turns into crystal clear water. It flows smoothly around me, and I can now see my feet. The shaking starts to subside as I place my arms around myself and hug my body.

Words start to form as the water gets less and less. It is so warm and comforting now, and I slowly sink to the floor, curled into the fetal position, cradling my knees up towards my chin.

Someone is talking to me in a soothing tone. I look around me. No one is there. Suddenly I realize it is I talking.

"It's over now. Let it go. Everything is going to be all right."

I roll over onto my back and stretch out my limbs. It feel so good as I start to relax, letting my thoughts run free.

"It was not your fault. These things happen to so many children."

"You can begin again right now, from this moment on. Make new memories that bring you joy and ease."

"But I can't do it on my own. I am too scared," I murmur back to myself.

"Yes, you can. Remember, you don't need anyone, and then of course there is Michael now. He is going to need you to be strong and take care of him."

Oh my God, have I lost my mind at last, now that I am free? I am talking to myself. What will people think?

"Who cares what people think. It never worried you before."

I smile to myself and get up off the floor. I feel lighter somehow, as if tons of weight has been lifted off my shoulders.

That's it. Today is the first day of my life, and no matter how hard it seems, I know it will get easier and easier every day from now on.

I have never shared this intimate side of my coming out with anyone before. I can see the eyebrows going up as people look at me quizzically, wondering if I have lost my mind. This was the day I created my favorite saying of all time and it marked the way to my newfound freedom.

When people hear me singing away as if I am alone, or I tell them I am whirling in a vortex of love and joy they often remark,

"You sound a little nuts to me."

And in my magnificence I answer as I have so many times before: "I may be, but I am the happiest nut you will ever meet."

CHAPTER 23

Thoughts Become

People often assume that because the child is not yet offering words, the child could not be the creator of its own experience, but it is our promise to you that no one else is creating your experience. Children emanate Vibrations—which are the reason for what they attract—even from their time of birth. Esther, Jerry and Abraham Hicks

As I LOOK BACK over the years, I see now how resilient I really was as a child. I had no idea at the time that what I was feeling could be changed by the thoughts I was thinking. I was too stuck in a religion that left me feeling powerless and hopeless.

Some people find it hard to believe that even as children we are responsible for the lives we are leading. You may ask how anyone would come into a life of so much pain and upheaval. I've asked myself that question many times as well.

Personal opinions are rife among the learned. Councilors and the like have had their information handed down to them over the years by people like Jung and Freud. I thought that as a councilor I would be able to help the children that I worked with confidently and professionally. The more I read of Freud's and Jung's theories, the more skeptical I became. According to them, almost every problem a child had stemmed from its mother and father. There was not much mention of religion, dogma, politics, and, most importantly, misinformation.

It can be daunting knowing that you are responsible for the life that you lead in every way, from the good and bad situations you find yourself in and the friends and enemies you have. However, it can also be empowering to know that whatever is happening, you can change just by the mere thoughts that you think.

Can you understand how empowering this could be for children of today? I have contact with so many children through the work I do, and the information taught to kids makes me wince.

I was told that if I were disobedient, I would burn in the fires of hell. This was described in such detail; I could almost feel the flames licking at my skin while I cried out for water to quench the thirst. Why would someone tell a young child stuff like that? It is such a shame that people who have such a so-called close relationship with God feel the necessity to use religion as a means to control the masses.

What about, if you don't study and go to university, you will never amount to anything? You will always be poor because all the money belongs to the well educated and powerful. You should be grateful for small mercies and not want more than your fair share.

Don't take the last cookie. It's too greedy. Give it to someone else. Don't be so selfish and think only of yourself. There are more important things in life than just you.

There is nothing more important in your life than you. You came here to live a life of fun while you discover through not wanting what you do want. Contrast is what gives credence to living. It is what teaches us about life from both sides of the spectrum: happy-sad, rich-poor, abundance-poverty. Without these contrasts, we can't know the other. Appreciation of the opposites goes a long way in the scheme of things.

If someone takes something from me now, or if a situation comes along that seems hard and unbearable, I do not react the way I did when I was a child.

Now I know that I can choose my reaction. Just as I did when they tried to take my son away and put him up for adoption. I had the answers. I was just blinded by the misinformation and limiting belief system that surrounded me as I was growing up.

In my imagination I could see my baby and me laughing and playing. Sharing wonderful moments together, growing up together. These pictures were so clear in my mind, I never had any fear they would remove my son from me again.

As soon as I released the past and its grip on me, the relief I experienced allowed me to connect with everything I am and all that I was becoming through my asking.

I was so confused about God, adults, and parents. I held on to things that were detrimental to my expansion and growth. This in turn held me back in life, keeping me in a place of fear and lack.

Had I been taught about my inner guidance system, I would have been able to choose my reaction to any circumstance, thereby changing the course of my situation.

Our heads are filled with such limiting thoughts and belief systems that we become powerless and flounder in misery and confusion.

I remember once reading a book, and although I don't recall the name of the writer, I do recall the one line from that book that stunned me: "Life is a banquet and half the suckers in the world are starving to death." The writer, of course, was not talking about food as such, but about life and all it has to offer.

There comes a time when you need to understand that no circumstances or situations can keep you stuck in a life or a place that you do not want to be in. Whether it be poverty, ill health, or unhappiness, by your thoughts and the choices you make, you keep yourself from moving on.

The privilege of reading books that could give me an insight into life's possibilities had been well hidden from me or banned in the schools I attended. Now, however, I had no excuse. I could make the effort to find out all the answers to the questions I had been asking. My perspective had changed, and so had my thirst for knowledge and enlightenment.

Everything I had known before became irrelevant to who I was becoming. I wanted to find out just how much control I did have over my life, how I could change without having to drown in past memories. I read about forgiveness, regression, and letting go. I started releasing the past.

If some past memory infiltrates my mind, I acknowledge the thought, thank it for the part it played in my life, and then release it. I am always growing and moving forward. My focus and goal is ever onward and forward.

It was time to let go of all those memories that held me captive, and then maybe I would be able to teach my son from a more empowering place. I did not want to raise him with the same limiting belief systems that had left me feeling so disconnected and alone.

CHAPTER 24

I am an Individual but not separate ¿I amî

I am magical physical extension
Of non-physical pure positive energy
Emotional vibrational perfection
On the leading edge of thought. Francine Jarry

NOW THAT I KNOW how to keep the feelings of joy spilling over into my life without the need for anyone else's input, I know that I am all powerful in creating the reality I desire.

It is not so much about negative or positive. When you feel good, you attract good energies; when you feel bad, you attract bad energies. You are all that there ever was and all that there ever will be. You are God Source in the physical realm. You came to have fun and enjoy life.

As you think, so you become, living every thought at one and the same time. You are thousands of thoughts at every moment of your life. There is no beginning and no end. Life continues on forever. You are infinite. You are constantly creating a vibration that keeps you walking the path of abundance or lack, of wealth or poverty, health or illness, happiness or sadness. Where you are now is where you chose to be.

You are forever part of the conglomerate of thoughts that you and everyone before you has assimilated. You live each and every moment by what you are thinking about. Everything is energy, and once the thought is expressed, it becomes a thing and that then becomes part of your reality.

Collective consciousness is like a grid of light beings. It is nowhere to be seen and yet everywhere. As you resonate, you emit a vibration that comes from your core where everything you feel aligns you with the exact same vibration. You create within your mind thousands of possibilities, and whether by design or by default you will draw to you the perfect match of each of those possibilities. You are not just you. You are all energy; you are a co-creator of unlimited proportions.

You exist endlessly in the parameters of all that there is. You vibrate on a level of divine love that knows no boundaries and no limitations. You are limitless; therefore you can do, be, and have anything. Unleash within yourself the abilities that allow you to design your life deliberately.

Your soul calls to you every moment of every day to join it in the dance and rhythm of this wonderful time-space reality.

When you are in that place of perfect connection with God Source, you feel good and pulsate like a beating heart, filling your being with such joyous harmony and moving you ever closer to your God Source. You can feel the warmth and glow as the vibration that emanates from God Source envelopes your being, gently bidding you to come hither. It promises you unconditional love and a most joyous reunion while still in this physical body.

You are connected to all things animate and inanimate, as all are there by your design. As you allow yourself to move through the many thoughts that fill your mind each day, you can judge them using your feelings, deciding which ones serve you well and which ones don't.

Your life is a whirlpool of emotions that warn you one way or another of which way you are heading. There is no right or wrong. If what you are doing or thinking brings intense feelings of love, empathy, and harmony, then that is the path most suited to your journey.

At every moment you can change your destiny just by your thoughts. There is no book of preordained chapters written for you. You are the creator of your existence here on this earth.

Everything comes down to the choices you make. Don't complain that if such and such hadn't happened, your life might have taken a different direction. The truth is and always will be that the only one who could have changed the path you were on is you. Even now you are not committed to any outcomes, and it is with confidence and clarity that you will find your own niche in life.

No one else is responsible for the way you respond to the things they are saying or doing. If someone makes a comment that does not feel good to you, then you need to ask yourself why you were there to hear that comment.

There is no such thing as coincidence. Every situation in your life is there by your design. You could try to remember what brought you there, or you could just let it go and find something nice to think about. If you choose to remain focused on the comment, it will further debilitate you because you allowed it too. Words are just that. They can't harm you unless you give them credence. Even so, they are merely the opinion of someone else and of no direct importance to your expanding life. You are source energy. Relish that fact.

The confusion that surrounds what and where source energy, or collective consciousness, is has given many people much food for thought. We think it is out there somewhere, and it can only be reached when we die. However, I for one am not prepared to wait until I die. I want to feel that connection now and know that I am always expanding and never ending. As humans we find it hard to believe in anything we cannot see or touch.

Thinking that perfection and happiness is only attainable upon death only sets you up for more disappointment. Ask the questions, for now is when you will benefit from using your feelings and looking within to find the answer.

Each night I would lie in bed and ask the same questions of God:

Who are you? Who am I? How can I define who you are and what you look like so that I can understand the concept of a god? The only emotion I received from this line of questioning was never enough. I wanted more.

Just feel your way into your own truth. What is there to know? Who but you knows what really rings true for you. This made sense to me, but surely there was more.

It was the early hours of the morning and I was still awake. In my mind I started having my regular conversation with God Source.

"I really am curious," I said. "Why, in all these years, have you never spoken to me? Who are you, and who am I?"

Suddenly I heard a car racing down the road at what sounded like tremendous speed. I was very familiar with the length of that road and also that at the speed the car was going it was never going to be able to stop in time at the junction. I lay there waiting for what I was sure was going to be the crunch of metal as the car lost control. Suddenly I felt very peaceful and the sound of the car speeding suddenly stopped. There was just a most beautiful silence and serenity about the night.

God Source answered. He said, "I am that car speeding by and the clouds in the sky. I am the leaf on the tree and the scrape on your knee. I am silence in the night and the sweet song of birds at daybreak. I am you and you are me. We are not separate. We are one. I am.

"Feel your way into your own truth. What is to know? Who but you knows what is true for you? I can be anything you want me to be, but most of all I am you."

Can you even begin to imagine what that means? "I am." We are past, present, and future. We are then and now. We are consciously and unconsciously connected to all that there is.

We are unique as humans but we are never separate. We are more than our personalities and characters. We are magnificent genius beings that are the extension of nonphysical, pure positive energy.

When another person brings to our attention something about ourselves that is not pleasing to them, we look at ourselves in despair. We begin to doubt who we are and allow them to make us feel unworthy. Sometimes we feel separated and wonder if we are flawed somehow. That is only because we have been taught that we should take into account the opinion of everyone else.

You see I believe we can never fall from grace. We are the thought form of God Source, always striving for perfection in our lives.

We are the physical extension of God Source, and therefore we are so deserving and oh so worthy of every consideration in this universe. Everything around us is energy. Nothing is solid, and that means you can change the energy around you to suit yourself by seeing yourself where you want to be.

CHAPTER 25
Self-Love

I am an expanding Being; I deserve more so I give myself permission to have more. My true state of being is Well-being. Linda Lang

"GIVE YOURSELF MORE FREEDOM treat yourself with respect and self-love, walk through life without guilt, and experience more joy and happiness." Abraham Hicks

These words had a huge impact on me when I first read them. I thought about them earnestly and wondered what they were really trying to tell me. I know what freedom means, but how does that relate to self-respect and self-love.

I used to think that if people did not like me, this meant I had to start behaving in a way that would meet with their approval. Then I remembered that as a young girl I decided that I did not care what people thought about me.

I used to detach myself from comments people made or what those comments implied. Most people prefer to conform to everyone else's opinions of them. For instance, I love to sing and I will do it all day long as it connects me to my God Source. I have been told by family members to pipe down, that my singing is embarrassing and that people are looking at me. I have a wonderful gift, which is my voice, and I use this gift with love and appreciation all day long.

You know what, I do not care. Anyway, most people would love to be able to just let go and sing when they are happy themselves, but they care too much about the opinions of others. This is where I found how self-love came into the picture.

I care more about how I feel than I do about what other people think. It is none of my business what they think or feel. Each person is responsible for how they feel. I had also discovered a new respect for myself. I was standing up for my right to be in a place of joy without the permission of everyone around me.

I had stopped catering to everyone else's need to be happy. I was living the life I wanted for me. I was going where I wanted to go, doing the things I had put off for so long because I thought they would disadvantage others.

Ah, self-love and self-respect. I was feeling mighty good about myself. Now when I looked in the mirror, I would say things like, you are the best, you rock, and I love you. The more I said the words, the more I realized they were true.

I was seeing myself through the eyes of Source or my higher self. I was indeed the perfection of life, and now I was starting to take notice of the things that made me happy. No longer was I concerned about making an impression on people. If they did not understand my total disregard of what they thought of me, I quite frankly did not give a darn.

The more I practiced this new way of being, the more I loved it and me. This love had nothing to do with the ego and everything to do with who I was becoming.

Suddenly I was remembering earlier dreams for my life that I had held so dear. I wanted to live them. I was over asking other people what they thought I should do. My life had nothing to do with them. This was about me, my dreams, goals, and aspirations. I wanted them all. It was not enough just to have one. If I was going to change, then it was going to be the whole hog. No half measures here, thank you.

And so I started the move out of my comfort zone. No more limitations, self-imposed boundaries, excuses, and complaints. Now was the time to release all old constraints and inhabit a place of my own design.

That is exactly what you do when you change your life. You rewrite the book, design new realities so that they fit in with your life. When you start to see yourself through the eyes of Source, you appreciate just how fantastic you really are.

I mean, look how your arms are in the perfect place for picking up things. Just imagine if your arms were behind your legs. You would have to stand on your head and spin around to get anything done. There is so much to appreciate about this wonderful shell that you have chosen to use during your earth experience.

You will be amazed at how fantastic you feel as you see how each and every part of your body plays its designated role. It does not matter who you are, what shape your body appears to be, and whether you have all your limbs or not. You are and always will be the perfection of life.

Source does not see missing parts, or overweight bodies, or scar tissue, or blemishes. None of these things resonate with who you really are or how Source sees you. When you look through the eyes of Source, you see with unconditional love, not just yourself but everyone around you.

The contrast in humans is there because we chose to come here to live. You need to appreciate that contrast. It will lead you to know what you do and don't want. As difficult situations arise in your life, there are two ways of dealing with them. You can feel fear, discomfort, and uncertainty, or you can feel love, confidence, and the security of knowing that everything happens for your highest good and expansion. I know which one I choose most of the time and which I prefer all of the time.

Ask and It Is Given, Seek and You Will Find

Everything is about vibration. When you feel confident and deal with contrast from the broader perspective (from the perspective of Source), you will raise your vibration and align with the solution to the problem without any effort at all. As we focus on the things we desire, we send out vibrational energy of that desire. Source becomes that which you desire, and then all you have to do is line up and receive it.

Many people say that they are lined up and they are sure of what they want. However, knowing what you want and then trying to receive it from the place of lack will never get you there. Once you ask for what you want, you have to trust and know that it is yours.

There is no need to start looking everywhere for it. Don't start ringing around, looking for it in elusive places and talking about it from a place of not having it. Believe it, see it, and receive it. It is that simple. I once read this little anecdote in a magazine, and it made me sit up and think.

A person says to God, "Every night I pray and I ask you for the same thing. I have been doing it for years now. How come you have never given it to me? Why don't you listen to me?"

"Well, my child," says God. "I did listen and tried to give it to you many times, but you made it so hard because you kept interfering."

That is exactly what happens. We ask, and then instead of trusting, we keep repeating our request from a place of disbelief. The law of attraction is the only law and it works from the vantage point of vibration.

If you are sending out desires while appreciating your life as it is, this raises your vibration. The universe can do only one thing: line you up with other vibrations to match yours and voila! There it is.

No hard work, no research from a vantage point of lack. The circumstances, people, events, and situations are now presenting themselves to you. They are coming faster than ever before, because now there is no resistance. You are aligned and milking the situations for all that they are worth.

Can you feel the excitement of this? Can you take it into your very core and harvest it? As you do so, you gain more and more. When I am in a good-feeling place, my day is filled with one moment after another of receiving that, which has been placed in my storage for all eternity.

Some things I don't even remember asking for, and I call these desires by default. As I appreciate and sing to the universe, she responds in kind to me. How good is that? Can you feel the power of that?

Sometimes we say, But so and so will be unhappy if I just do what I want. Well, let me tell you, if you take into account all the unhappiness of every person you come into contact with because of something you did, when do you think you would ever get to do, be, or have anything for yourself? Do you think that you came here to cater to the need of the masses? Do you think you can make the world happy by having less for yourself?

This would mean that there is only so much money or abundance to go around. Nothing could be further from the truth. There is endless abundance and prosperity for everyone. You came here to have fun, to feel good.

Any time you feel uncertain, hook into your feelings and ask the question. Take note of how it makes you feel. If it feels good, do it. Don't ask your family what they think. Simply trust that when you share your decision with them, they will be thrilled for you.

Enjoy your newfound independence and milk it, milk it, milk it. Learn to trust your own opinions, and when you share them with others share them from a place of feeling good. Amazing things will start to happen in and around your life. Do not worry about losing your friends. They will benefit greatly from your happiness.

You will soon make new friends who are vibrating at the same level as you are. You will find that when you share your time with them, they will elevate and help in your expansion.

CHAPTER 26

See what you want to see
Look for the positive aspects in every situation.
Words to a song written by Francine Jarry

IN MY LINE OF work, I get to meet many people from all walks of life.

One day a couple walked in, and they both looked so miserable. She kept telling me that they wanted some particular pavers, but they wanted something cheap. She kept indicating that they didn't have any money to spare. However, I felt somehow that the place they were in had nothing to do with their lack of money.

My intuition was telling me that it had something to do with their neighbor's. They had that look of confusion and unreasonable frustration that a bull with a ring through his nose gets when he want to join the beautiful cows, but you keep leading him away.

"So," I said, "your next-door neighbor's music is getting you down, I see."

They both looked up, stupefied at this knowledge coming from someone they had never met. I don't as a rule read minds or even consider myself to be psychic, but there it was.

The man grinned sheepishly and nodded. I felt so appreciative that I might be able to help. You see, not that long ago I was having the same problem. My neighbor figured himself to be a pop star and would play this music, which sounded like a bass drum, all the time. I was going out of my mind, and even closing the windows made no difference. I love to sing and have the same feelings of grandeur that my neighbor has about his star status, so I sang to counter his music.

So there I was, singing at the top of my voice, trying to drown him out. After about a week, I felt disempowered by all this. I decided that something needed to be done, only I was not quite sure what. As I looked out my kitchen window, pondering this dilemma, a beautiful little boy appeared in their backyard. He was smiling to himself and seemed so happy with all the noise.

There you go. I had sent out a vibrational desire about my preferences, but still kept pushing against the thing that was not wanted. Instead of relinquishing my need to try to find an action that could bring me satisfaction, I continued to stress over the situation.

As I watching the boy, a sense of relief washed over me, as if a heavy weight had just been lifted off my shoulders. I was in such a wonderful place simply from witnessing his contentment that I capitulated and let the feelings lull me back into my sweet spot, as I call it. I also noticed that even though the music was still playing, I was putting my own words to it and actually enjoying the beat.

I smiled happily to myself and felt empowered by my ability to find such a good-feeling place just from letting go of my need to control someone else's life. Moreover, my neighbor no longer plays music all night, and when he does play it, he turns it down to a pleasant volume.

All I had to do was surrender to my true desire to live in a peaceful environment and allow the universe to bring it to me.

After I related my story to the couple, I could see that what I had said made sense to the man, but I got the feeling that his wife did not agree.

Sometimes well-meaning family and friends think that through their interference, they are helping us. The truth is, they are not, and when we don't take charge of a situation, we are relinquishing our power to expand spiritually.

There is always a solution, and you just have to go with the feelings of your guidance system. If you are dealing with the situation from a good-feeling place, you are no longer pushing against what you don't want.

Releasing the need for control will place you in that beautiful cosmic whirlpool where all cooperative components exist. When you reach for relief then, you will feel so much better. From that place you will begin to break free from the shackles that enslave you.

Your happiness does not depend on what someone else is doing. It depends on your relationship to you. That means nothing and no one has more relevance to your expansion than you do.

Well-Being Abounds

Looking at life through the eyes of Source keeps you in a place of non-judgment. When you see life through the eyes of love you will be bombarded with evidence of more of the same. Linda Lang

We play games of helplessness and blame every day. We constantly shirk our personal accountability to ourselves by trying to hold other people culpable for what is happening to us. Each time something happens that leaves us frustrated and confused, we say that someone else is responsible. This is just an excuse; no one can ever think your thoughts for you.

What has really happened is that we have forgotten who we are and the purpose of our being here. As we assimilate all the different belief systems into one of our own, it becomes like a game of Chinese whispers.

By the time our belief system reaches our subconscious mind, we have created a path to follow that forms a sort of distancing between our God Source and us. We listen to the radio and watch TV and then add fear to the equation, along with distrust, anger, and guilt. We start to feel guilty that we have food on the table and people in third-world countries have none.

One day a friend of mine was regaling me with a story of her holiday in Indonesia. She was almost in tears as she told me about how poor the people were there. She said that she felt so guilty about having this expensive holiday, and drinking and eating so well every day.

I was interested to see just how guilty she really was feeling.

I asked her, "If you had known about this issue before you spent all the money on your holiday, would you have given up the chance to go to Indonesia?"

"God, no," she retorted. "It's not my fault that they have nothing."

"Did they tell you that they had nothing?" I asked.

"No. Actually, they always seemed so happy to help in any way they could. I never once saw anyone without a smile."

I then asked her if they complained about any lack and she said no.

You see she could not understand why they were so happy even though they appeared to have nothing. It was only nothing according to her standards, not theirs. They were appreciative of their circumstances. They were not blaming her or anyone else for their lives; they chose to be where they are. What my friend failed to notice was that all the money she had just spent on her holiday in fact matched up with other vibrations and desires that had been launched into the universe.

This money was creating jobs for some people, putting food on the table for others, and boosting the economy around her from every angle. If she had given up her chance to have a holiday, nothing would have changed for these people. They would have continued to benefit from other people who have no qualms about spending the money they had earned in order to make their lives more comfortable and exciting.

So please don't think that if you forego the pleasures of life because you feel guilty about your abundance and other people's lack of it, that it will make any long-term impact on their lives. The only person who would suffer would be you, and all because you feel guilty.

Throughout your life you have probably heard people say that if you think of yourself, you are selfish. What is selfish about taking care of number one? You came here to this time-space reality to do just that. You never said you would come here and take on all the troubles of the world and her people, so that you could live in misery until you died.

How wonderful that you have the means to share your wealth with those around you. How fantastic that because of you, people have jobs and food to eat, schools to go to and books to read. Feel good about what you are doing, and I am sure those people in whose country you are spending or donating the money will appreciate it more and more.

You came here with the express intention to make your life a most joyful and exciting experience. You came here from a place of utter contentment, love, and abundance to see if you could replicate that existence on earth.

You are not just a human in flesh form; you are also at the same time Source Energy thinking you into existence. Wow, how utterly cool is that. Can you now begin to understand the power that you have and how excellent a co-creator you are?

When I think about it, it makes me want to do the wild stallion guitar riff like Bill and Ted did during their excellent adventure.

When I was little, adults would scold me for not eating all my food. They would say something like, "There are children all around the world that have no food and you are wasting yours."

Do you see how our belief systems are so corrupted by handing down the same beliefs from one generation to the next? Those people were trying to make me responsible for the hunger of the world. It was not my fault that those children found themselves in the circumstances they were in.

Give with love and from the heart because it is what makes you feel good, not because you feel guilty. Whenever the Earth expands and we are inundate with floods or earthquakes, humanity automatically comes together to help and support one another. We know we are connected and we love to share our abundance.

When you look for the positive aspects in a situation, you will see the benefits to those on the receiving end. If, however, you only see the negative, you will be given more evidence of that.

Feel Your Way

Oh, this is a good one, learning to use something that each and every one of us was born with. The moment we come into this world, we begin to lose sight of our precious guidance system. It is the one true emotion that will never lead us astray.

You have your own emotional guidance system. It tells you when you feel good or bad in relationship to what you are thinking or doing.

If you are going for a job interview, trying to decide on the best course of action in a new situation, going on holiday, or even just deciding to purchase something, your guidance system will give you an indication of how you really feel about what choice you are about to make.

Time and time again I hear someone say that he had to do something he did not like doing. I mean, really, why would you do it then? You are under no obligation to listen to anyone else's demands. No one is holding a gun to your head, and even if they were, you still have the final say in the matter.

You either like doing it or you don't. You simply cannot blame someone else for your decision to go ahead and do something that goes against all that you believe in. Doing something you don't want to do is like giving away your reason to live. You only came here to do what you want to do. Throughout the years people have been blaming one another for the wars, environmental destruction, diseases, and anything else that they can fight against. I have never heard anyone say that they made an informed decision not to get involved in someone else's reality.

I constantly get e-mails from organizations asking me to join in some fight against terrorism or whaling or to save the polar bears. People do not yet realize that the more you push against unwanted things, the more apparent they become as part of your reality. All those energies giving credence to more unwanted things makes those things escalate. Eventually you feel so unhappy about them, you can't live in abundance because you believe you are taking something from someone else.

Is it not wonderful that we have choices, and we can make these choices from a place that makes us joyful? Does it ever occur to people that those whales chose to be here in this time-space reality, and that their expansion is now complete and they wish to remove themselves from our human existence?

Do you wonder why they are beaching themselves in the thousands? Can anyone really talk for the whales? Are these people so orientated to marine life, they understand the complexities of the sea creature's expansion? I think not, and therefore it makes sense that we continue with our evolution and allow the creatures of this earth to enjoy their own evolution.

And that is exactly the point. You have the final say when it comes to making your choices. If it does not feel good, then don't do it, period. Allowing is the greatest gift we can give to all who reside on this earth.

Do not go around blaming your decision on the president or a senator or a king. Yes, they can attempt to persuade you to do something against your wishes, but they cannot force you. You are the master of your mind and the captain of your soul. If you choose to go along with something that is distasteful to you, you are not being true to your self.

Always be true to you. Feel your way around; savor the pleasure when you discover your power in really knowing your inner self. That is why your emotional guidance system provides you with feelings of empathy, love, kindness, consideration, and appreciation. In light of these emotions, you are able to draw the same matching vibrations back to yourself.

Don't be afraid to heed the warnings of your guidance system, for it will never let you down. Take the time to test it out by going ahead with a plan of action that you have in mind or that dream that has been shelved for so long. However, be sure that you never put before you a challenge that is unbearable or too difficult to complete. When you feel good, you are lined up with source energy and nothing is impossible.

Do everything that you do from the perspective of source energy and you will never have cause to say words like "If only I had . . ."

There is also nothing wrong with being selfish, as you did not come here to work out the lives of others, only your own. After all, what other people get up to has no bearing on your life whatsoever, unless you allow it to

If you take to heart what others say or think about you, you will have to live your life according to what makes them happy. Immediately you become a slave to their rhythms. You start to choreograph a life pattern that takes into account the likes and dislikes of everyone around you. Your life becomes so complex, and you forgo all the things that make you feel good in order to satisfy their whims. One of the most misleading concepts of all time is that you are responsible for the feelings and happiness of others.

You know who you are and where you fit into the scheme of things. You need not be afraid, only excited at the prospect of sifting through the buffet of variety life provides and finding out what resonates with you.

From a place of love, go with your feelings. Ask yourself questions and see where they take you emotionally. No hemming and hawing; just take the bull by the horns and do it.

Don't ask members of your family how they feel about it, or your friends or the neighbor. It's none of their business. This is your life. You want to find where you fit into the scheme of things, not them. It is your dream to fulfill, to go there, say it, do it, and feel it.

The moment you ask someone else to agree with you, you are saying, here is my life control it. Decide for me what I can and can't do, whom I can and can't love, where I can and can't go.

Do you see how that removes you from all that you are and puts you in a place of hopelessness? Your life is your own; no one has the right to tell you what is best suited to your reality.

Don't ask someone else what a color is. Look at it, feel it, and then give it a name. That is all it is, a name seen through the eyes of someone else. Everything in our lives is about feeling.

As you concentrate on revaluating your life and belief systems, you will find that you have less time to interfere in the lives of others. What other people do will become irrelevant to your personal expansion, and you will notice little things happening that will start to align you with your desires. You will begin to understand your connection to all that there is and realize that happiness does come from within.

Shakespeare wrote, "All the world's a stage/And all the men and women merely players." Focus on this for a bit and let your imagination run wild. Can you begin to understand the power in these words? In fact, you are the writer of the story that you live and you can change the direction of the plot whenever you want. Let your chapters give evidence of the journey you most desire. Write your book of life as if it were a movie script and then live it.

How often do you smile at a stranger? Do you ever greet someone that you don't know? I have actually heard people say that some person was not worthy of them, just because he looked a little scruffy. How easily people criticize each other or place others in different categories. No one is better than another.

We are all God Source and connected. Take the time to share the love around. See everyone through the eyes of Source. I can promise you this: in the eyes of Source, we are all perfect.

When you see something that displeases you, look the other way. There is no law that says people have to change their behavior to suit you. The longer you focus on that unwanted thing, the more prominent it will become in your life. If you don't want that, then just ignore it and it will go away. It has to. That is the law of attraction, and the law states that you will only ever line up with what you resonate with. Change your vibration by thinking good thoughts that feel good.

Are you tuned in, taped in, and turned on to your feelings? Do you make excuses for why you can't go here or there or do this or that? Whenever I hear people say those things, I understand immediately why they never seem to get anything done. Why they always seem so unhappy. They never take the time to just go with their feelings, and their excuses are simply a way of making something or someone else responsible for their lives. Take charge of your life and become a match to all that you have accumulated through your asking.

I am the Master of my thoughts and the Captain of my Soul. I am ready to expand and grow so that I may be all that I can. I know that there is no shortage in the world and that I am a magnet, attracting abundance, prosperity, good health and Wealth. I am always provided for and so I never have to worry about the lack of anything. Linda Lang

There is never a reason to deny yourself pleasure of any kind. If you desire something with all your heart, give yourself the freedom to ask for it. All you have to do is imagine it, pretend it, and believe it. Don't go running around trying to find it. Stay in the vibrational equivalent of that desire and it will match up with you. You deserve the very best in life, so make it your proclivity to have whatever you want.

You are a co-creator, and by merely thinking about something, you make it become. Can you imagine all those thoughts floating around out there finding another vibration like itself to attach to? Here is the fun bit. Think thoughts of unconditional love and appreciation, and watch as the universe brings more of the same to you. Are you beginning to see the power that you wield?

Awesome, is it not?

Be the master of your thoughts and find ways to inspire yourself into elation.

Trusting and Letting Go

In order for me to love myself I need to let go of all previous restrictive thought patterns. I am an unlimited Magnificent Genius Being. I see myself through the eyes of love. I draw to me healing and comfort as I gently make the changes in my life that I need to become empowered again. Linda Lang

These are the precise words I used to help me let go of the past. Growing up in a series of orphanages created plenty of baggage. The longer you hold onto memories like those, the trickier it gets to release them.

Often we think we did not ask for the hurt, but in actual fact we did, only unconsciously. You see, we are so used to just thinking thoughts indiscriminately that we are hardly even aware of some of them. They sort of swim around in our heads in reaction to things we see or hear.

More often than not I hear people say, "I can't help what I think. It just comes automatically, so I have on control over my thoughts." In fact, you can control the thoughts you think. Every one of those thought patterns is residue of experiences you have had. Let the thoughts run free and take notice of how you feel about what you are thinking. If what you feel is distressing and disempowering, then it is up to you to acknowledge the thought, thank the experience that created it, and send it on its way. Look at who you are now and how strong you have become because of the experience. Don't try to analyze it. Just accept it and let it go.

As you release all the old hurts and pains that have held you captive, you draw nearer to Source. You can always tell when this happens, because you feel so overjoyed at what is and nothing or no one can distract you from that place. You are the perfection of life. Every day you make choices that create a better life for you.

Look at Life through the Eyes of a Child

I am excited about the changes happening in my life, I am talking the talk and walking the walk of my spiritual connection to Source and all that there is. My vibration is high and the Law of Attraction is lining me up with my desires. Linda Lang

Spending time on your own, appreciating and enjoying your own company can and will give you the time you need to get in touch with yourself. You can take time to redefine who you are and what your purpose is in this lifetime.

Whenever there is a breakdown of a partnership or even a friendship, many things about that relationship come to light. Often you realize that when it came to giving, you seemed to be the only one doing the giving or sharing or compromising. Now it is time to give back to you. Let there be no more compromising. As far as I can see, compromising just means you have to give up your wishes and dreams to suit someone else.

Never ever give your power to someone else. Never feel guilty about anything you do if it serves your personal expansion and growth.

If only you could see life through the eyes of a child. Children trust without question that their every need will be provided for. They do not judge people by color, creed, or religion. There is nothing they cannot do, be, or have as far as they are concerned.

They love you no matter how you look first thing in the morning and kiss you on a mouth that to you tastes like a birdcage. Their love is unconditional, unprejudiced, and directly from God Source.

They love themselves as if they know that they are the most important person in their lives. Their worthiness is not even a question, and they will eat almost anything without the slightest worry that they might put on weight or that the food has too many calories. They never fear sickness or anything of a lower vibration.

We are the ones who come into their lives and teach them that they are limited, and that there is evil and bad in this world. Unfortunately, we also then indirectly create a reality for our children that consists of fear, prejudice, untrustworthiness, and conformity. They begin to take on our belief systems.

Is it any wonder that most children are so healthy and happy, even ones in third-world countries? Children are so precious, and we need to take a leaf out of their books. There is the magic of their imagination that can take them to any place or situation they want to be in.

These are the things you need to remember about yourself. Take back the magic, become inspired again, and take action to allow good-feeling thoughts fill your mind. You are in control of your thoughts and your life now.

Tell yourself, "Today is a new day and I am starting my new life. I release the need to have other people change their ways to make me happy. I am the only person that can make me live a joyful life. I respect the right of other people to follow their bliss, and this gives me more time to pay attention to my own life." Linda Lang

Tell the Story

> *I am the Choreographer of my life's plan, the more details I see the easier I create and the more I can reach for that good feeling thought. I know that the quickest way to manifest my desires is to focus on the end results and believe. Linda Lang*

The reason we say, live your life deliberately, is because that is the only way in which you can be in harmony with you. For too long we have given the media and other people control over our reality.

Each morning without fail, the media come up with the worst possible news they can and regale us with all the sordid details. If you are a news watcher, that is pretty much what you will think about and talk about most of the day.

That's one for the media, none for you. Then during the day you hear more news on the radio, someone tells you a nice juicy story about a coworker, and you find a new scratch on your car.

All this is living life by default. You think a thought, and you think a thought and . . . that is how the whole day goes while someone else is creating for you.

I do things that inspire and pleasure me. I deserve to be spoilt, and I buy myself beautiful things without worrying about where the money is to come from. It is my money, so I will spend it as I see fit.

Become a deliberate creator and, oh boy, what power you will wield. I always say that I am the director of the Greatest Show on Earth and I am vying for an Oscar.

What kind of story do you tell every day? Do you do it consciously or unconsciously? Do you constantly repeat the same things over and over about your love life, bank balance and bills, and how they all lack substance? The more you tell it as you think you see it, the worse it becomes.

Tell a story of a wonderful soul mate and the dream home you share, with a robust bank account and wonderful investments that pay fantastic dividends each day.

This is where the magic comes into play and you get to feel like a child again. Let your imagination run wild. It is your show; you are the writer, director, and producer.

Live your stories, and introduce friends and neighbors into the equation. How about the car you have always wanted? What about that job that you have dreamt about since you can remember? You know, the one where you have an office way above the city with the most stunning views. The best boss in the world who is part of your social circle, with a house in the country or at the beach or both. Go crazy. Design a life that is exclusive and opulent or simple and quiet. It is entirely up to you.

Dream up a Caribbean cruise or trip to Hawaii. There are no limitations because it is your story. In order for your desires to come true, you have to feel the emotion of this dream. You have to live it as if it has already come true.

You are aiming for the highest vibration that is the identical to the story you are telling, so as to get the perfect match. Let there be no doubts in your mind about the authenticity of your desire. See it, believe it, receive it, and the universe has to bring it to you. It is the law.

Be a person with discernment. Choose what you observe and know that the best way to change the scenery in your life is to look the other way, or find a better-feeling perspective of the situation. Nothing is ever as it seems. There is always another perspective.

Remember that there are no coincidences in life. Everything and everyone is there because of your asking. So always ask for the best and expect it. Believe that you are worthy of the highest consideration from the universe and you will receive it.

When you have found the way to make yourself feel good, you raise your vibration. As you think, so you become. You are a being of light, capable of manifesting all your dreams and desires.

Life is fantastic, and you only have to be appreciative of all that you already have to raise your vibration and allow more of the same into your life. Live each moment and savor it as if today is all that you have and the pleasure that you will derive from it will keep you in that place called your sweet spot.

Whenever I have to make a decision about my life in any way, I trust my emotions to guide me to the perfect solution. There is no wrong or right for me, just what feels good.

I can use my imagination to pretend that I am healthy, abundant, and wealthy. All I need to do is feel my way there and the universe will line me up with it. You can fool the subconscious mind into believing anything you want. Don't let the ego butt in and tell you that people will think you are nuts. Who really cares what they think? It is your thoughts that count and which will bring you to your greatest good.

Modern science has proved that everything in our world is made up of energy. Even though your car, house, bed sheets, and even your hand appear to be solid, they are actually made up of energy and light.

All these energies also vibrate at their own frequencies. A lower energy cannot attract a higher energy and vice versa.

Food for thought, hey? As for thoughts, they too are energy. Makes you want to take control of those runaway thoughts of yours. Also makes you wonder why no one said anything about this before. Vibration is another word that no one wanted us to know about. Apparently we are not ready for it. Strange, but it did not scare me when I first found out that our lives are comprised of energy and vibration. If we use them consciously, we can live a life of empowerment.

We would then be able to match up to a higher vibration and, hey presto! Any wonder that those in the know have kept it such a secret for all these years? Here I thought there was a shortage of everything, and that only a few who were smart enough to be rich were entitled to it all.

I have lived my life from both ends of the spectrum. Over the past thirty years I have read more books on enlightenment and empowerment than I have had breakfasts. I have taken from each book what resonates with me and built new and joyful memories.

When I tell a story from where I am now, I tell it to the exclusion of all others. I allow them to tell their story, have their opinions, and create their realities from their own perspectives. Therein lies true freedom.

I move past the boundaries that I have created for myself with negative thoughts and limiting beliefs. I now allow myself to follow my dreams and live my life guilt free. It Rocks to be me. Linda Lang

Now the "Secret" is out there. It is a secret no more, and just like the genie from the lamp states, "Your wish is my command," so says the law of attraction.

A New Beginning.